Lightning Moments

Lightning Moments

WITHIN SECONDS, LIFE CHANGED FOREVER...

Focus ∘ Believe ∘ Achieve

Devri

Devri Ficklin

ISBN-13: 9781542680325
ISBN-10: 1542680328
Library of Congress Control Number: 2017900987
CreateSpace Independent Publishing Platform
North Charleston, South Carolina

"Devri's story stayed with me. I was discussing *Lightning Moments* with my daughter, and she immediately read its story for herself and then used the story in a competitive motivational speech. The book's message is accessible to youth and adults, whether they are committed goal setters or are just starting on plans to change some aspect of their lives. Best of all, *Lightning Moments* encourages readers to keep their priorities straight along the journey to self-improvement. It's a rewarding read!"
—J. J. LYON, FORMER JOURNALIST AND AUTHOR OF
TRUTH IS RELATIVE: A TRUTH INDUCER MYSTERY

As a new mom juggling a busy work, home, and social schedule I often struggled to focus on the right things. The systems in *Lightning Moments* allowed me to see my own power, and to take control of my life to become my very best.
—D. HOLDAWAY, WIFE, MOM, PROFESSIONAL WRITER, BLOGGER

Contents

Preface

Struck by *Lightning*, I survived!

Life seemed to be on track when within seconds, a lightning bolt, out of the blue, changed life forever. The emotions of this memoir resonate as you experience this engaging story of trials and triumphs that include recovering from a devastating divorce, family death, suicide, and disheartening financial struggles.

Lightning Moments is an electrifying story that allows you, the reader, to experience the destruction of a lighting strike and the recovery firsthand. While implementing the systems shared in this book, I endured months of painful healing—learning to walk, talk, and even *think* again—and emerged the victor not only surviving a lighting strike but thriving because of it!

Discover the little-used fact—you become what you do repeatedly. By intentionally and consistently using the systems shared in this book, you too can build a successful life and achieve your goals through three simple actions: focus on productive thought, embark on a journey of peace through forgiveness, and make each day count by managing your daily actions.

Lightning Moments is the first of a two-part self-help and leadership series designed to inspire the reader to get life "back on track" when tragedy shows its face! It's more than just a story of survival and triumph over an actual lightning strike. The motivational stories encourage the reader to improve personally, each day!

Enjoy the journey!

Devri Ficklin
LightningMoments.com

Acknowledgments

t will never be enough for me to simply say thanks to the many people who encouraged me to write this story. The story has taken many years to "live," and the amazing saga of life continues. I express my gratitude to those who have played a huge part in crafting this memoir.

I appreciate the thousands of students and staff of Paul Mitchell Schools across the nation who inspired me to put the story into words.

I am deeply grateful to the late Dr. Kocherhans for his patience and wisdom and to Valerie Demick for her extensive knowledge. Both of them taught me how to heal by focusing my thoughts.

Special thanks go to Jodi Wonacott, a true friend who, using her talent, organized this book and activities in a way others would understand; to Molly Quirk, who assisted in creating the beautiful images and graphs that made the book an interesting read; and to Jill Law, Gail Fink, April Hanrath and Danica Holdaway, each helped me in some way to put the indescribable experience into words.

I thank each and every one of my children for their support in using the systems to achieve happy, successful lives. My kids are a true inspiration to me.

Finally, but certainly not least, I acknowledge my sweet husband for his unwavering love, support, and encouragement. Without him, I might never have completed this book. He is my best friend and the love of my life, and I am extremely blessed to have him by my side, today and forever.

CHAPTER 1

Lightning Moments

Within Seconds, Life Changed Forever!

t's like an exclusive club, the "Lightning Strike Survivors." Of the nearly eight billion people on earth, only a small percentage is actually ever hit by the electrifying force; many do not survive. Of those who do, most do not remember the actual strike. I do! This is my story.

Lightning Moments

We all experience them: Lightning Moments, those pivotal events in our lives that change everything. They come with the death of a loved one, a divorce, a job loss, a tragic accident, or the birth of a baby. These moments offer a unique opportunity to look inward and ask, "What am I to learn from this?" When devastation crashes in, you have a choice: improve or stay the same.

Everything was right for that warm holiday weekend. Pine Valley boasts of aromatic pines, shimmering sun, cool breezes, and peaceful seclusion from the outside world. My husband, Don, rolled the windows down as we neared the campsite. We breathed in fresh, woodsy air and the scent of a distant campfire. But the beautiful surroundings were nothing compared to the sight of our family cheering our approach.

"Uncle Don! Uncle Don! Come see!" Our nieces and nephews practically pulled him from the truck when it finally rolled to a stop. Tents dotted the campsite, as most of the family had arrived the previous day. But the party didn't start until Uncle Don arrived.

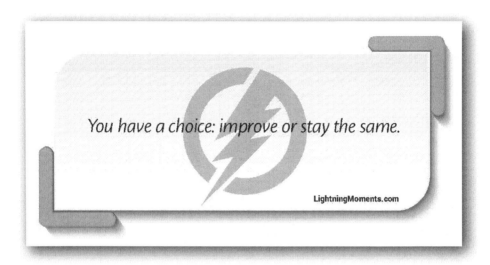

You have a choice: improve or stay the same.

LightningMoments.com

"We saved that area for you." Don's brother motioned to a flat space of ground. It looked perfect, and Don would set up the tent in a few minutes, after he joined the excitement. I jumped in to help with dinner. Tonight's meal would be authentic spicy jambalaya (the recipe courtesy of Great Grandma Malbrough, handed down through generations of our Louisiana Cajun family). It was the perfect start to a fun weekend.

It felt good to be with family, and we enjoyed a delicious dinner, talking and laughing the way you can only do at an annual family reunion. A warm summer shower surprised us before we could have dessert. Typically, you can see a storm brewing as it cascades down the canyon, but not this time. It felt different as the sprinkle fell instantly from tiny clouds, sharing the sky with the bright sun. The women and small children huddled under the canopy for shelter from the warm droplets. Don and the boys, unaffected by the random rainfall, continued to set up the tent no more than fifty feet away.

And just like that, a few minutes later, the shower stopped. The hustle and bustle quickly resumed around our campsite, with the summer storm all but forgotten. I again began to clear away the food, with the warm sun on my face and the scent of the damp ground in the air. The light streamed through the towering pines, and everything felt fresh and bright. As I lifted the edge of the Dutch oven, I became aware of something dark looming at the edge of my vision high above my head.

I lifted my gaze to take in the ominous gray cloud. In that second, a deafening boom engulfed my senses. A thin ribbon of blinding light emerged from the darkened cloud, followed by a watery, transparent, dancing blur of energy. It leaped toward the tall trees not more than fifteen feet from where I stood; it was thin yet jagged, spreading its tail of vibration. The top of the tree suffered first, and then the light and energy spiraled down the trunk in a fiery ring. I stood in horror, struggling to stay on my feet, hearing, feeling, seeing, smelling. A huge puff of smoke and fire billowed up, and bark scattered to the ground.

It wasn't immediate, the recognition. The rapid seconds of this event were stretched out by shock and pain into a perceived eternity. *It's lightning*, I thought. *I am being struck by lightning!* The realization spread with the excruciating burning in my hands. I was unable to lower my head, but by lowering my eyes, I could see my hands. They looked like a cartoon, the bones a visible shadow through peach-lit skin. The terror spread as every muscle in my body continued to contract, as though it was seizing, folding in on itself. It felt tight, immovable, agonizing.

Nothing could prepare me for the torture of the second bolt of lightning. It racked my torso, crushing the air from my lungs, the intensity ramming through to my spine. I could feel an intense, surging, zigzagging golden energy through my core, ricocheting off organs and bones. The pulsing seemed endless, and it hissed within my ears as it raced from hands to feet and back again.

I felt an electrifying surge as the bolt concentrated its strength within my torso, building, intensifying. Then it began its gradual ascent toward my heart. The end would come soon. Unable to speak, I cried out within my mind, *Help! Please help me!* Instantly, it felt as though a pair of hands entered my chest and protectively encircled my heart. The beating never stopped. Though fast and scared, the heartbeat was strong and never skipped a beat. The energy from the lightning swarmed up and around my heart, continuing on its path. Relief came only for a moment, as I realized the surge would soon reach my brain. There would be no defense.

Time seemed to slow down. What took only seconds seemed to last for minutes, as memories and thoughts of my husband and family flashed through my mind, crippling it with the sorrow of loss. Don and I had married only four wonderful years earlier, a second marriage for us both; our newest grandbaby would arrive in a little more than two months. Dying would mean I'd miss out on life's experience. My husband would need to tell the children of my passing. That thought racked me with grief. I'm too young; I do not want to miss life...

Lord! Please help me! I do not want to die!

What happened next is difficult to describe and even more difficult to believe, but I lived it. I didn't hear the words, at least not with my ears; I felt the words within my whole being. Someone I felt I knew yet did not recognize, someone who knew and loved me, said, "Her body has had enough." I then felt him quickly place the heel of his hand against my forehead and push as he said, "Get her out of there." The pressure from his hand propelled me from the field of energy that consumed my body. I felt myself falling through blackness—and then nothing.

Open Your Eyes!

The lightning strike naturally caused chaos and panic in our campsite. Everyone searched for their children; they were disoriented, stunned from the blast, with ears ringing and children crying. Eventually someone noticed me and yelled, "Devri's down!" My husband ran to my side. Piecing the stories together, I later learned I had been thrown up and over the propane stove, landing some fifteen feet from where I originally stood. I lay unconscious in the fire pit.

My memory is of darkness. The world was silent. Slowly, I became aware of someone cradling my head. "Baby, oh, baby, open your eyes." I could hear concern in Don's voice.

What's happening? My thoughts felt like a blur. As hard as I tried, I could not move my body.

He pleaded again, "Please...Baby, open your eyes."

Gradually, the memories returned. *Lightning!* I couldn't believe it; I was alive. Yet, as much as I willed myself to open my eyes, I had no control over my own body. Don continued to plead for me to respond. I could *feel* the devastation in his voice. My heart clenched in pain. He believed...I was dead. I must *move*. For him, these moments had to have been filled with torment and grief. Praying, urging, I tried so hard to open my eyes, but to no avail; my muscles would not obey.

Frantic, I began to play the scene within my mind. In slow motion I opened my eyes and propped myself on my elbows. I pushed to a sitting position and then slowly lifted off the ground and floated up and out of my body. I turned to look directly into my own face. My body still lay on the ground, just a few inches away, so close I could feel the warmth of my own breath on my skin. My eyes were closed. *Please, open your eyes*, I pleaded. No response. I could see Don cradling my head within his hands. My heart felt his sadness. I had to do something. With every bit of internal energy I could muster, I took a deep breath and then strengthened my plea. I yelled directly into my own face, *Open your eyes! He's going to think you are dead!*

I felt light flood into my eyes. They were open! Dazed, I slowly became aware of the ground below me, cold and hard. My legs and arms felt hot, heavy, and fatigued. Everything seemed fuzzy, but nonetheless, my eyes were open.

"Oh, sweetheart!" I could hear the joy in my husband's voice. Through blurred vision, I could see his face as he smiled with relief, the shadows of people clustered around in concern, and the jagged top of a tree. Then confusion set in. *It's snowing. Oh, wait, no...That's bark from the tree...and ash, struck by lightning. Oh, right...so was I.*

Though my mind was active, my thoughts and body could not keep up. My brother-in-law, a doctor, assessed the situation. I tried to speak. *My hands...my feet...I can't move.* The words came out in an unrecognizable slur; my tongue felt swollen in my mouth. Don and his nephew, Brent, tried to help me stand. I immediately collapsed. The family felt it would be best to seek medical attention. Don offered a special prayer on my behalf for strength before we took off. Although I was still unable to move and my speech was limited, I recognized the spiritual stamina offered to me through this prayer. I knew I would survive. It would not be easy, but I would survive.

The twenty-five-mile ride into St. George was unbearable. After being carried to the car, I spent the trip in throbbing pain. I tried to speak, urging Don to take me back so this wouldn't ruin the family vacation, but he resisted my garbled plea. The unique pain combination of pulsing, pinpricking sensations and numbness was absolutely miserable. Though I tried not to cry, tears rolled down my face. The prickling sensation was constant. My hands and feet began to burn with heat. As they began to swell, I remembered I was wearing my brother's wedding band, which he had given to me before he passed away. This ring was all I had of his, and if they had to cut it off my ballooning finger, I would be inconsolable.

I had to get it off. I raised my hand and watched it flop wildly. My fingers snatched and grasped at the ring like a giant arcade claw, unable to precisely fix onto the ring and remove it. Finally, using both hands, I lifted my finger to my mouth and, using my teeth, slid the ring off safely. Though horrified at my lack of bodily control, I felt gratitude for being able to preserve this precious memento.

At some point, memory loss set in. Feeling the burn in my hands as if for the first time, I turned my gaze to Don, and in slurred speech I asked, "What happened to me?" I searched his face for some meaning as my arms quivered from unexplained pain. Don patiently explained the lightning strike and our ride into town to the hospital. Within a few minutes, my memories of the strike returned. The sequence repeated itself again a few minutes later.

Just outside of St. George, we met a police officer. He summoned an ambulance for the final ride into the hospital. Despite my efforts to contain it, I cried out uncontrollably from the pain caused by the careful transition from the truck to the ambulance. Once I was inside the ambulance, the paramedic assessed the situation. He asked a series of questions, and though my memory seemed clear and vivid, I was unable to communicate well. My slurred speech made me difficult to understand, and I often forgot midsentence the answer or the questions the paramedic asked. By asking a series of yes or no questions, he was able to receive the most accurate answers from me. I remember one question clearly, though it made little sense at the time.

"This may sound a little crazy. As I lift your shirt, please look down to see if you notice something that looks like a spider's web on your chest."

Although confused, I complied, looking down my shirt for what I imagined would be a white, spindly spider's web. Instead, I saw leaves and bark from the tree, but nothing that remotely resembled a spider's web. As he continued his assessment, he asked if I remembered the path the lightning took through my body. I pointed to my hand, my arm, and then down to my feet. Then I remembered.

"Hit here, too," I slurred, and I motioned to the aching spot on my torso, near my right ribs. He gently lifted the bottom of my shirt to reveal the spider's web. Rather than a white and dainty web as I'd imagined, it was a violent red-and-purple mark, with two- to three-inch welts reaching out like the threads of a spider's web. He soon found the initial bruising on my back, where the second lightning strike had passed completely through me; swollen and red now, it would soon grow dark and painful.

The hospital was a complete blur for me, and I remember very little of my time there. My husband said the doctor had to research online for lightning-victim care, because I was the first lightning survivor he had ever treated. Unfortunately, he found very little on patient care. He opted to perform a barrage of tests to ensure that all my internal organs were in working order; the tests showed nothing significant, and only time would tell. Slowly, speech control began to return, but memory did not follow. Instead, my short-term memory loss appeared to get worse. I couldn't carry on a conversation or remember things that had happened just a few minutes before. A swishing pain—like static electricity was traveling back and forth deep within my muscles—continued relentlessly, up and down, back and forth. The painful sensation of pins and needles in my extremities seemed permanent.

Contemplating Life

It's commonly mentioned that individuals see their life flash before their eyes when they experience a near-death episode, and this was certainly true for me. I lay awake for most of that first night. I was unable to sleep due to the persistent ache deep within my entire body. I was fighting the short-term memory loss, my thoughts kept coming and going, and my mind was occupied with the scenes that flashed before me; thoughts continually reliving the path of the lightning within my body and of losing my family. I couldn't help but think, *What if I had died?*

Before the strike, I was finally happy. I had a wonderful marriage and I took great pride in our beautiful family. I enjoyed a successful and fulfilling career. That night in the hospital, fear swelled within me. The thought haunted me: *What if this had been the end?* No one is ever ready to die. But, if the lightning strike had killed me, I would have left a slew of things undone. I knew deep inside that I wanted to achieve more, so much more.

A terrifying thought that I had faced death—yes, I should be dead, yet for some unforeseen reason, I was still here, still alive. I had so much more I wanted to accomplish before I died. My thoughts turned toward God, and I expressed gratitude. "Thank you," I whispered, grateful I had lived.

But...*why did I?* Lightning strikes usually kill people, yet I had lived. *Why me?* The realization settled on me softly: I had been given the gift of another day, another chance to get it right. And I would not waste a minute.

Time to Begin Your Journey

It required a life-changing Lightning Moment for me to take inventory of my life and discover that my potential was much greater than my current achievements. Great success was my destiny, and with a plan and consistent action, I knew I could achieve it.

LIVE your potential — now!

LightningMoments.com

What about you? I implore you to live your potential, now! Never wait for a Lightning Moment before you take action to improve your life. Learn from the experience of others. Over many years, I have had the exciting opportunity to share this message with thousands of people. Many of them have applied the systems shared in this book, and they too have enjoyed personal success.

Create Your Own Lightning Moment

The first step is to look at your own life in slow motion. As lightning wrenched my body, the seconds felt like hours. Scenes from my life, my family, and my job played out before my eyes. I discovered changes I wanted to make.

Now it's your turn. Think about your everyday life, your family, and your friends. Visualize your home and community. Contemplate your career, hobbies, and other obligations. What makes you happy? What is causing you stress or maybe even guilt? If today were your last day how would you want to spend your time? Are there things you wish you had completed? Are there relationships in need of creating or in need of repair? If your life flashed before your eyes, what would you see? How would you feel?

These thoughts and feelings are indicators of the health and happiness of your life. Even if you live an incredible, joyful life, it's likely that you still have feelings of regret or things you want to accomplish in order to achieve your true potential. On the other hand, if your life is miserable and you feel that nothing is going right, you would see many things that need to change. Now is your chance to *be* the lightning by creating a Lightning Moment. Identify what you're missing or where you want to grow. Then make it happen.

Life Reflection: A Perfect Day

Take a moment to reflect on your most perfect day. Ask yourself, "If I were living the last few months of my life, what would I choose to do? Who would I call or connect with, and how would I want to spend my time?"

Record your feelings by identifying the individuals and activities that are most precious and important to you. What would you regret not having accomplished? Is there anything or anyone you need to connect with? Write your thoughts on the "A Life Reflection, A Perfect Day" activity sheet provided in the "Knowledge in Action" section at the end of this chapter. Visualize and then record how you would describe your most perfect day.

Chapter 1
Lightning Moments
Within seconds, life changed forever!

Knowledge in *Action*

LightningMoments.com

A Life Reflection, A Perfect Day

Visualize and then record, how you would describe your most perfect day. Explain the day in detail. We will refer to this a little later in the book.

CHAPTER 2

Motivation versus Inspiration

Motivate Yourself First, and Then You Can Inspire Others!

M otivation and *inspiration* are two words often used interchangeably, but their meanings are very different. Motivation is not inspiration, and inspiration is not motivation. Yet the two words work together; one can help perpetuate the other. Now that you have identified how to create your own Lightning Moment, let's discover how to use motivation and inspiration to achieve success.

Inspiration means "in spirit." It lifts your emotion and frees your mind. You are able to see and feel things more powerfully. Inspiration can come from many different sources, such as music, movies, books, nature, and other people. Inspiration is important because it allows you to see potential that would otherwise seem impossible. Inspiration creates excitement and expands horizons. But that's all it can do. Inspiration does not cause you to *do* anything. For that, you need motivation.

Motivate yourself first, and then you can inspire others!

LightningMoments.com

Motivation comes from the word *movement*—movement that relates to both inner motion and outer motion. It's the process of getting started and heading toward a goal. Motivation is what you *do* with the inspiration you feel. You can watch an incredible movie about another person's struggle and triumph and feel inspired, but the only way to turn that inspiration into *your* success is to motivate yourself. No one else can do it for you. *You* alone must take steps to move toward your goal. Motivate yourself first, and then you can inspire others.

Lauri, My Friend

I am useless, I thought, tears streaming down my face as I sat on the couch. It had been nearly a month since the lightning strike, and I had lost both motivation and inspiration. Slowly my memory became stronger, yet my body was weakened. I felt depressed, with no desire or energy to move forward or even try. Moving was laborious and sloppy. Numbness and pain tingled in every limb. *I am supposed to be the one who cares for others*, I thought, torturing myself. The realization that memory loss and paralysis were now a way of life haunted my every thought. *Am I destined to depend on others for every simple need?* It felt suffocating. *I can't* live *this way!* I clasped my chest, struggling to slow down. Panic set in, and every breath became a battle. My lungs were slowly being squeezed, and I simply couldn't get enough air. Fear ruptured inside me, and I grabbed the arm of the couch in a panic. I wanted to leap from the couch, but I couldn't. *Will I ever...feel...normal again?* I screamed within. Life as I knew it was over. An audible plea tumbled from my lips: "Please, oh please, help me."

Then the memory of a dear friend came to mind.

My thoughts drifted back to a period about eight years before, when desperation and depression had controlled my life. I could see the time clearly in my mind, as if I were living it again. I lay sprawled in bed, unmoving, though it was nearly afternoon. Panic and dread struck as I realized the kids would be home soon, meaning I must get up and make some dinner. *Ugh...I simply can't* live *this way!* I had a disease that plagues so many individuals: all-encompassing depression topped with a bit of self-pity. For years, I was dependent on anxiety meds, but they weren't working. I just couldn't shake the depression. It felt as if I couldn't get a breath, so I wrapped my arms around my chest in an attempt to hold myself together. I paused for one slow, deep breath, and again tears began to run down my face. Then the phone rang.

"Hi, Devri!" The voice sounded cheery yet strained. It was my friend Lauri. We hadn't spoken for a couple of months, but I was happy to hear from her.

"I need to have surgery, and I'm looking for a substitute teacher to hold my position." She worked as a cosmetology instructor at Paul Mitchell Schools two days a week. "It would only be for a couple of months, while I recuperate. Could you work for me—just until I can return?"

My heart sank. I wasn't sure I could help. Lauri had no idea I was struggling with my own challenges. Daily I searched for any glimmer of happiness. For years, I had worked to build a strong family, yet I spent nearly every waking moment consumed with the fear of losing everything I had worked so hard for. I was in the middle of a messy, difficult divorce. At that moment, the fear of being a single parent and having to provide for my family by myself seemed too much to bear.

Putting aside my personal concerns for the moment, I said, "Lauri—share with me. What's going on?"

"It's not a big deal," she began. "Remember the tumor I had removed from my spine five years ago?"

"Yes," I replied, instantly concerned with the direction of this conversation.

"Well, it's returned, but the good news is the tumor is encapsulated." I could tell she was trying to be brave. "The surgeon is very confident he can remove it with no lasting side effects." She shared a few more concerns that could include paralysis but concluded with, "I have a really good feeling about this. Two months and I will be back to work!"

Her treatment would include surgery, radiation, and three weeks of chemotherapy. This should stop the cancer, and after two months of recuperation, she was confident she would be back on top.

As I listened to Lauri talk about her life-threatening struggle, my troubles seemed to pale in comparison. Throughout my adult life, though I had run my own salon in my home for seventeen years, I had focused mainly on raising my kids. I had not taken the time to really build a career.

Now emotionally stressed because of divorce, I struggled with having the energy to even *think* about my career, let alone build one. I spent more of the day in bed than out. How could I work two days a week in the school? To do so meant I would have to get out of bed for longer than thirty minutes at a time, something I had not often accomplished in over two years. It seemed hopeless, but I desperately wanted to help her.

With a huge prayer for strength, I put my life's woes on hold. "Yes, my friend, absolutely I will help you."

Lauri gave me the inspiration to get out of bed through her example of determination. Her friendship meant everything to me. Knowing that in a heartbeat, she would do it for me became the driving force that would motivate me into action.

Surely, I could put my personal challenges aside for a few hours a day to help her during her recovery.

I began working at the school two days a week, fighting through my depression, inspired by my friend. Before Lauri returned to work, healthy once more, I was hired on as an employee of the school. This gave Lauri and me the opportunity to work together two days a week for several wonderful years.

An Inspiration to the End

Four years later, I watched Lauri's body wither away as she battled bone cancer, one surgery after another. The cancer returned to her spine for a third time. To everyone's relief, her doctors had removed the tumor that had wrapped around her spine. But six months later, they found more cancer, this time in her humerus, the large bone in her upper arm. This led to a second operation a year later, followed by radiation. Each time, the doctors assured Lauri that they had successfully removed the cancer.

One day while she was at work, Lauri mentioned that her left leg felt sluggish and painful, so she was going to visit the doctor again. Within a week, the doctors discovered that the cancer was back, this time in her spine for the fourth time. Over the next few weeks, Lauri's body weakened to the point that she was forced to use a wheelchair, and soon she was completely reliant on others for everything. A month later, Lauri was unable to move from the waist down. During one of my visits, she asked me to adjust her legs as we sat on her bed. I bent down, bracing myself to lift her legs. But they were feather light, practically nothing—just saggy skin, thigh bone, and very little weight. Without use, Lauri's muscles had quickly atrophied.

It seemed impossible. Within three short weeks, Lauri had gone from walking, running, and riding her mountain bike to needing a wheelchair and depending on others. During the next few weeks, I visited her daily to help pass the time. We talked about the adventures we would go on when her health improved, such as riding our mountain bikes and taking a scenic Harley ride. Lauri drove her own Harley, and she couldn't wait to get back on it. During one visit, I brought my new haircutting clippers, and we discussed a new cutting technique we were learning at work. Lauri asked if I would help her learn the new skills so she'd be up to speed when she came back.

"Yes," I said, "I'd love to! It will be fun."

Later that day, as I left for home, Lauri's mother asked me to join her in the living room. Out of Lauri's earshot, her mom asked, "When Lauri passes, will you do her makeup and hair?"

I was shocked. "Of course I will. When…the time comes, I will be happy to do whatever is needed."

"Devri, Lauri is dying. We need to make plans now."

"No, that can't be true. Lauri and I are making plans for when she gets better and returns to work."

"Devri, the cancer is growing so fast that she will be gone in just a few weeks."

As I left Lauri's house that day, tears filled my eyes and sadness filled my heart. I had had no idea she was in her last days. She was so inspirational, always focusing on what we could do and never dwelling on what she had lost. I cried all the way home.

Only a week later, Lauri's husband called to let me know she had passed peacefully in her sleep. I still treasure the four years we had together working at the school. Lauri remained a positive and inspiring force until the very end. She helped me get through the emotional final few years of a complicated divorce that seemed to drag on forever. I hope I helped her through her final few weeks of life. I will always cherish our friendship and her love of life. Because of Lauri, I was able to move forward, and my memories of her would inspire me to do that again and again.

Questioning My Destiny

As I sat crying on the couch five years later, it seemed selfish to compare surviving a lightning strike to Lauri's life-threatening struggle, yet the memory of her battles, her loss of mobility, and her reliance on others for every tiny thing raced through my mind. My situation was totally different: I was not deteriorating due to a body-ravaging disease. But I thought of how quickly Lauri's muscles had weakened without use.

Wiping away tears, I looked down at my forearm. Muscles that had been strong and toned before the lightning strike now sagged; the skin and muscles seemed to hang off the bone. The intermittent paralysis from the lightning strike made every movement challenging and laboriously painful. Frustrated, I felt trapped in a body in rapid decline, and the deterioration weakened my spirit. I didn't want my body to wilt; I didn't want to stay dependent on others for my basic care. To keep my muscles strong, I had to sprint. I had to keep moving!

My friend Lauri was a remarkable individual. Never once, no matter how challenging her health issues, did I hear her complain or give in to the disease that engulfed her body. Her inspiration lifted my spirit that day as I sat on the couch recovering from the lightning strike. It was as if I could hear her on the sidelines, waving her sweatshirt above her head like a flag, cheering me on along the road to recovery. "Keep moving,

I will accomplish this goal...
one small step at a time!

LightningMoments.com

Devri! You can do it!" I took a deep breath to settle my fears, wiped away the tears, and then took action. I knew what needed to happen, and it would take motivation, or in other words, movement—one small step at a time to achieve my goal.

I looked at my feet as I visualized the inspiration of my good friend cheering me along. "Come on, body," I said as I wiggled my toes. "We will not give in!" I didn't want to just *dream* about walking without assistance. I had a goal: to get on my bike and ride. I would accomplish this goal, one small movement at a time, and it would begin with my toes!

Your Inspiration and Motivation

Take a moment to analyze your desires and your potential. What lifts your spirit? Your inspiration is something that makes you feel that anything is possible, like my visualization of Lauri cheering me on. Next, identify your motivation. What action will get you moving forward toward your desires? Finally, what is keeping you stuck?

Is there one specific goal you would like to accomplish but have been putting off? Write this goal in the space provided on the "Motivation versus Inspiration" activity sheet in the "Knowledge in Action" section at the end of this chapter. Then reflect on your actions, and record your answers to the next two questions: What is keeping you from moving toward your goal? And what is one small action you can take that will begin the forward movement? Once you've identified it, take action and do it!

Chapter 2
Motivation vs Inspiration
Motivate Yourself First, and Then You Can Inspire Others!

Knowledge in *Action*

LightningMoments.com

Motivation vs Inspiration

Take a moment to analyze one specific goal. Write it in the space provided, and then record any actions that keep you from achieving that goal. Choose one small action you can take that will begin forward movement towards achieving the goal. Once identified, take action and just do it!

Goal

Action – Movement towards goal achievement

CHAPTER 3

Action Plan

Live the Life of Your Dreams!

W alt Disney's Cinderella reminds us, "A dream is a wish your heart makes." A dream is something hoped for, a desire to achieve. I believe a dream *is* just a wish—that is, until you write it down and take steps to make it a reality. The simple act of writing down your dream draws fulfillment closer. In my experience, as soon as you identify your dream by writing it down, the forces of the universe will begin to assist you in making that dream a reality. This chapter is designed to help you discover the early steps that can help you move toward your goal. Take the time to define your dream, create a step-by-step process, and begin moving toward your deadlines and checkpoints until your dream becomes reality.

Action Plan: Five Simple Steps to Goal Setting

After the lightning strike, it took me time to identify a real, achievable goal. Once I finally decided that to "ride my bike" was what I really wanted, my goal was clearly defined. Then came the reality: a long list of challenges to overcome. That meant that my dream would remain a dream unless I designed a plan. Five main steps lay ahead, and I used them to achieve my goal:

1. Identify your goal.
2. Consider possible challenges and solutions.
3. Actualize (visualize and affirm) goal achievement.
4. Outline tasks and actions.
5. Set checkpoints and deadlines, and share with others.

Step 1: Identify Your Goal

Cycling is something I love to do. Although I had a strong desire to ride, the lightning strike had robbed me of that ability, at least temporarily. I had little control over my motor skills or even my mind (my thoughts bounced around, and I rarely completed a full sentence). I certainly couldn't balance a bike. But I knew that achieving this goal would represent my personal triumph over the lightning strike: the impossible made possible!

I began to visualize riding my bike, and I thought back to my first experience of balancing a bike on my own. I was eight years old, and I rode a beautiful candy-apple-red 1969 Schwinn Stingray, with a banana seat and a rear handle for assisting new riders. My cousin Rod ran alongside the bike, holding the handle on the seat to help me balance. He cheered me on: "Come on, keep going. You can do it!"

I remember clearly the exhilaration I felt when, for the first time, I balanced the bike on my own. Rod shouted, "Yes! There you go! Keep going!" He released the bike, and I rode the length of the street in front of our yard. In the years to come, I learned to ride and steer with no hands. I could float my arms high into the air, gliding to the left, then to the right. I felt on top of the world.

As I became an adult, my passion grew. After Don and I married, we invested in a nice pair of bikes and began riding casually around our neighborhood. We built up our endurance and our ride time, from two to three miles to five or six miles to even fourteen-mile rides on the dirt trails behind our Las Vegas home. Finally, we decided that we would train and prepare for a long mountain bike ride near the family cabin in Pine Valley. We worked incredibly hard that spring to build strength and endurance for the twenty-three-mile mountain ride. It would include many uphill climbs, thrilling downhill rides, twists, turns, and most of all, gorgeous scenery.

One month before the lightning strike, Don and I took that incredible ride, and I can still feel the crisp morning. The air was chilly on my hands that day as we coasted out of the cabin driveway at 6:30 a.m., facing the six-mile uphill climb before the sun came up, hot and strong. Scenes of deer, rabbits, birds, singing brooks, lush trees, and flowers flash through my mind. I remember feeling my hair flowing as the wind rushed by.

Now my heart sank as thoughts of never again experiencing that mountain ride entered my mind. I thought I might never have the body control to balance a bike even on a stable, flat road. The thought was crushing. I knew I couldn't—no, wait—I *wouldn't* take that disappointment. I would ride my bike again. Even though I couldn't do it right then, I would ride that mountain trail again. I would use my vibrant memories of that mountain ride to sustain me in the months to come. This would be my final triumph over the lightning strike.

I had identified my goal. When I had ridden my bike, I had felt pure joy, and I wanted to feel that again. I knew exactly where and how I wanted to do it.

Step 2: Consider Possible Challenges and Solutions

With my goal identified, I started on my plan with excitement. However, limited control of my motor skills would present a significant challenge. Not only did I need to develop the strength and endurance to take that mountain ride again but also I needed to accomplish every tiny step between—on the one hand, simply walking again and, on the other hand, riding dozens of miles on a mountain road. I started with the first challenge: rolling my ankles, which at that moment was all I could do. I began spending hours a day focusing on rolling my ankles in every direction until I could perform the action without thinking. Then I moved on to knee lifts and calf lifts. I knew I had to work up to standing, then walking, running, and eventually riding my bike alone. Those were the challenges. The solution consisted of daily work, exercise and movement, and the encouragement of others.

Step 3: Actualize (Visualize and Affirm)

The next step is to actualize, which is a combination of visualizing and affirming. I learned this step from a smart gymnast.

In 1984, all eyes were on Mary Lou Retton, a tiny American gymnast competing on the global stage in the Summer Olympics. In a sport long dominated by athletes from communist countries, American gymnasts finally had a shot at an all-around individual gold medal. When Mary Lou's final event drew near, I watched the television broadcast breathlessly. I had been a gymnast in high school, and though I was now twenty-three with three small children, my heart was beating in my throat for her, my favorite gymnast.

She raised her hand, nodding quietly to the judges. Then she was off, pounding down the runway toward the vault. When she reached it, she flipped flawlessly through the air, propelled by the springboard into the electrified air. Planting firm and sure, she struck the landing perfectly and threw her hands up. Seconds later, she was awarded the elusive perfect ten! There was no need for a second vault, but she returned to the starting position. She would prove to the world, with a second perfect ten, that she had earned and deserved that score. It was no fluke; it wasn't luck. It was hard work.

Almost twenty years later, I found myself face to face with my idol, Mary Lou Retton, when she was a guest for the Children's Miracle Network telethon in Orlando. Though I was emotionally downtrodden and depressed from my impending divorce, meeting her was a bright and shining light.

I asked her a question she'd been asked many times before: "What were you thinking the day you stood at the end of the vault, knowing the weight of winning the gold rested on your shoulders?"

Though she had given this response thousands of times over the years, she answered me with passion and courage, as if it were the first time. "I knew I was prepared, for I was taught to visualize the outcome. I knew I could do it!"

She went on to explain that six weeks before the Olympics, she had suffered a devastating injury to her knee that required surgery. The surgery was a success, and she was able to walk almost immediately. Though her training would be limited, she began working again one week later. During the recovery, she often visualized her Olympic performance as she lay in bed. Over and over, she would visualize each and every event—a perfect performance from beginning to end. She cheered herself on. She even visualized standing on the Olympic platform and receiving the gold medal while the American flag was proudly raised and the national anthem honored the US champions.

Now as I sat on the couch, unable to do much more than wiggle my toes and roll my ankles, Mary Lou's story inspired me. Even if I could not physically ride my bike, when I visualized the activity, in my mind it was real. I would use visualization and affirmations as a way to increase the speed of my physical recovery. I would see myself riding my bike on that mountain pass to Pine Valley, lifting each knee and then pushing the pedals down with energy and vigor along each mile.

Visualization helped me in two ways. First, I avoided dwelling on what I could not physically do at the time; second, the excitement of my anticipated bike ride kept me energized. I pictured every mile along the ride. I imagined the tightness of my quads and hamstrings as I pushed the pedals, one at a time, up the long six-mile hill from Pine Valley to Grass Valley. I felt my calves burn, and I mentally down-shifted the gears on the bike to make the pedaling easier. I imagined it early in the morning, with the sun just peeking over the mountains. I felt the crisp breeze blowing through my helmet, keeping me cool during this tough section of the ride. I worked for hours, reliving the ride and tightening the muscles of my arms and legs as I played the movie within my mind, pushing each pedal down, one at a time, and gripping the handlebars for leverage as I repeated the affirmation "I can do it! I am healthy. I am happy. I am *alive!*"

Step 4: Outline Tasks and Actions

Riding my bike was the ultimate goal, but physically achieving it would require many little steps along the way. I made a detailed list of the steps and actions I needed to take to achieve my goal. Besides moving my limbs, they included standing, walking with a walker, taking excursions from the bedroom to the kitchen without stopping to rest, walking with the use of a cane, and finally walking unassisted. I knew that it would be weeks, possibly months, before I could try to ride my bike down a quiet street, followed by several more weeks or months before I could achieve the big goal of making the beautiful twenty-three-mile mountain trek from Pine Valley toward Enterprise. With my list of goals and solutions in hand, I wouldn't give up.

Gradually, it became easier to rotate my ankles and wrists without much effort. The next step would be to control my knee movement by lifting my knee, tightening my calf muscles all the way down to my toes, and then slowly extending my knee and pushing through the ball of my foot as I visualized the pedal, one pump at a time, on the long and steep gravel hill out of Pine Valley.

Once I perfected the pedaling movement, I moved on to tackle a more difficult task: standing alone. The fear of falling hung over my efforts, and it took energy to focus my thoughts. I visualized the activity and encouraged myself out loud, beginning the first attempts to stand using the bed for leverage: "Come on...you can do it! I am brave. The bed is there to catch me!"

I felt like a small child learning to go down the stairs for the first time. I started by dangling my legs over the edge of the bed. Then, rolling onto my stomach, I stretched one foot ever so gently, extending my leg until I could feel my toes touch the carpet. Next, holding on to the bedcovers, I extended my other leg until both feet rested comfortably on the floor. With my arms, I would lift slightly off the bed, extending my back while leaning my tummy against the bed. I held this position as long as I could, tightening the muscles in my legs. Then, when my legs or my back grew tired, I'd lie back down on the bed and rest. I performed this exercise over and over, as many times as I could, until my legs were shaky and weak from fatigue or my back just couldn't take the pain any longer.

Some days were better than others, and it was a daily struggle. I made it a routine to begin with actualization, which included imagining the activity and cheering myself on. Then I would move. What began as small twenty-second bed lifts—balancing on my legs, with my thighs and stomach leaning against the mattress—grew into one to two minutes of holding, which then grew into pushing my stomach away from the bed and holding myself up with my legs all on my own. I celebrated every little task I completed, every step to success. "Yes! I did it! I am strong! I am amazing!"

Step 5: Set Checkpoints and Deadlines, and Share with Others

As I pressed forward with my task, the struggle became easier. Progress and celebration were internally motivating, and they kept me moving forward. Each day I scheduled time to review my progress, adjust the list of tasks accordingly, celebrate every little achievement, and determine the next step of my journey.

As I press forward, the struggle becomes easier!

LightningMoments.com

After practicing "bed standing," my next step was to walk. I would push away from the bed slightly and shuffle around the bed. I overcame my fear of falling by seeing the mattress as my safety zone. The bed was always there; if I needed to, I could quickly lie back down. Tears of joy filled my eyes the first time I stood, pushed away from the mattress, and took a few steps. "Three small steps for Devri, one giant leap toward walking on my own!" I imagined myself as the astronaut taking his first walk on the moon. Maybe I wasn't leaping yet, but I celebrated nonetheless.

When I had built enough arm strength, I decided it was time to try using the walker. I found it much more difficult than I had anticipated! I felt lost without the security the mattress had provided. I made my first attempts with my husband or daughter right by my side. They encouraged me. "Come on, you can do this!" As I held tight to the handles of the walker, they would take my arm to lift me to a standing position. My first steps were slow. With each step, piercing sharp pain began at my toes and fingers and radiated up my arms and legs. It felt like I was walking on pins and needles. My right side was sluggish; I had to concentrate on dragging my right foot into position. I knew that if I didn't get that foot under me, I would fall. Every step required an all-out effort.

When I was alone, I strayed very little from the comfort and security of my mattress. Over time, I built strength and could push off the bed by steadying myself with the walker and no other assistance. Still, every time, I had to control the little voice inside my head that wanted me to give up: *It's too hard. It hurts. Stop. Lie back down!* I consciously had to replace these thoughts with actualization to focus my mind: *Yes, I did it! I took four steps this time! Great job!* I continued to visualize and affirm, celebrating each little success along the way.

Finally, with continued practice, I strengthened my arms and legs and could use the walker for more than a few steps at a time, each day moving a little farther from the bed toward the bedroom door. The movement, however, felt slow and painful. With each step, a pulsing rush of energy moved back and forth, back and forth, as if a tidal wave of blood rushed from my fingers, up my arms to my shoulders, and from my toes to my hips. It took every ounce of courage to keep moving. Relief came at the end of the workout, with a leg massage from my sweet husband, Don.

Soon my husband and daughter reluctantly returned to work, leaving me home alone. Don worried about me, and though I didn't tell him, I worried too. I barely left the safety of the bed or couch without him there. He thoughtfully placed chairs every couple of feet throughout our home, and I could use them for balance or to rest as needed whenever I ventured off the couch with my walker.

After achieving the goal of walking with a walker, my next step was moving with a cane. Then I moved to walking without assistance, and finally I began to ride my bike on the quiet streets of our gated community. My original goal was to be back on my bike by my birthday, but that gave me only three weeks, which proved to be an impossibly short amount of time. I could ride at five months, but it took pretty much all of nine months and many baby steps before I felt comfortable balancing a bike in traffic. Though I worked at it daily, nearly a year passed before I achieved riding my bike again on that mountain road.

Goal Achievement

Finally, the day arrives. As we navigate that mountain road, sports-induced asthma begins. I suffered asthma and bouts of pneumonia many times throughout childhood, and I've often given in at this point due to fits of coughing and tightness in the chest. It feels as if I've hit the wall. Fear takes over. *Stop! Stop now! I can't breathe...* Thoughts of overwhelming exhaustion fill my mind. It would be easy to give up. No one would blame me. I can't breathe; my thighs and calves ache. Quitting would be easily explained. *For heck's sake, you've been struck by lightning...It's OK; just stop!* my thoughts pleaded.

Then I think of Lauri on the sidelines, and I think, *No! It's not OK.* Willing the child within to fight back, I take control of my thoughts. *You—no, we—can do this. Do not give up!* Pausing for just a moment to breathe a puff of albuterol into my lungs, I begin pumping the pedals again and reciting an actualization mantra: *I am alive. I love to ride! My body thrives. It feels great to exercise!* Again and again, I repeat the affirmation with enthusiasm and commitment. I feel the adrenaline kick in, and the tightness of my chest and legs lessens.

Although the journey was difficult and long, both Don and I never gave up on the dream of riding our bikes again on that beautiful mountain road, and the achievement of this goal made for an exceptional day!

It takes consistent effort, but the payoff is worth it!

LightningMoments.com

I am often asked, "Are you one hundred percent healed?" The answer is no, and I probably never will be. However, I have been given the gift of another day, and I do everything I can to make the best of this wonderful life. Yet this is just the beginning.

Throughout this book, we will learn how our thoughts control our actions, how peace comes through forgiveness, and how daily actions determine our success. Achieving dreams takes consistent effort, but the payoff is worth it. *I am alive and living my dreams!*

What about you? What is your dream? If you could be, have, or do anything you desire in life, what would it look like? What is your goal? Write it down. Avoid putting it off until the "right" time; record it now. Once you identify your goal, you can begin making your dream a reality. You deserve to realize your potential and achieve your goals—become all that you are destined to be.

Recall the goal you identified in the previous chapter 2, "Motivation versus Inspiration." Take a few minutes to expand on that by completing the "Five Simple Steps to Goal Setting" activity you will find in the "Knowledge in Action" section at the end of this chapter.

You will develop this information throughout this book as you create a detailed "action plan." Are you ready to create the life of your dreams?

**Chapter 3
Action Plan**
Live the Life of Your Dreams!

Knowledge in *Action*

LightningMoments.com

Action Plan

Identify your goal and then complete the Five Simple Steps to Goal Setting activity. Put your plan into action as you take each small step towards goal achievement. Take the time to share your success with a friend who can help to hold you accountable for checkpoints and deadlines.

Five Simple Steps to Goal Setting	
Identify Your Goal 1	
Consider Possible Challenges and Discover Solutions 2	
Visualize and Affirm Goal Achievement 3	
Outline the Tasks and Actions For Goal Achievement 4	
Set Checkpoints and Deadlines, Share With Others 5	

CHAPTER 4

Dynamics of Thought

Claiming Who "I am...!"

M aster your thoughts; they create your reality. Success comes when you focus your thoughts on what you want to achieve. Thoughts affect feelings, and feelings influence actions. If you allow your thoughts to wander, they will follow the path of least resistance. After the lightning strike, I found myself drowning in thoughts of loss, a mind-set that drew even more loss into my life. Replacing these negative thoughts with positive ones became a vital step toward my recovery from depression. Neither quick nor easy, recovery didn't happen overnight. Learning to focus—to channel a mind-set—on productive thought made all the difference in recovery. Another phase of my journey will help to explain the "dynamics of thought."

Success comes when you focus on what you want to achieve.

LightningMoments.com

At sixteen, I married my first husband. Though young and inexperienced, we worked hard to build a happy life together. But in the end, we both wanted very different lifestyles. During the last ten years of marriage, we spent more time apart than together. The breakdown of our marriage threw me into a personal struggle with a deep clinical depression, which finally led to the demise of the marriage. The gloom of depression is very difficult to explain; it is much more than just sadness. Depression is the inability to see happiness; instead, life is dreary and is filled with dark dismay, bone-chilling coldness, and an absence of any peace of mind.

Suffocating

One night before the divorce from my first husband, as I lay alone in bed chasing sleep, thoughts rushed through my mind. I envisioned myself sitting on the edge of a steep, rocky cliff, with a raging sea surrounding me and the night, cold and dark. I sat alone. There was no way up and no way out except through the cold water. *I'm not a good swimmer*, I thought in panic. I could taste the salty air as the waves crashed around me. Slowly, I pushed forward and slipped into the deep-blue sea.

An image of drowning filled my mind as I began to sink into the chilly water. I held my breath for as long as possible, and then survival instinct took over. I tried to push toward the surface, and I felt the pull of the undertow and pressure on my lungs as I sank deeper. Flinging my arms upward, I gasped for air, and my lungs began to fill with water. I couldn't breathe. *Where is the surface?* As hard as I tried, I couldn't reach it.

Then the dream ended, and I returned to the safety of my bed, where I lay defeated. Tears slowly slid down the side of my face and puddled in my ears. *It would be so easy...In fact, it would be better for everyone if I simply slipped away.* That night, I methodically planned an end to this suffocating existence. In despair, I could see no other way out of the bleak, painful unhappiness.

Fortunately, the next day I had a visit with my family therapist, whom I had been seeing professionally on and off for a few months. I had met Dr. Kocherhans twenty years earlier. Our children attended the same school, and we had crossed paths many times. Several months earlier, during my first separation, I had begun to see Dr. Kocherhans professionally. Over time he had earned my trust, and I was able to tell him my thoughts from the previous night about ending my existence. He did not try to talk me out of the plan; instead, he reminded me of my two children, who were still living at home. He patiently and respectfully asked some tough, thought-provoking questions in an attempt to help me understand this most important message: our thoughts affect our feelings, and our feelings influence our actions. I was the protector of these precious teenagers, and Dr. Kocherhans had me envision their devastation over the death of their mother.

"OK, let's plan for the kids. With you out of the way, what would happen to them?" he asked. "Who would take care of them?" Dr. Kocherhans reminded me of my grandchildren and those not yet born. Grandchildren who would grow up without ever personally knowing Grandma Devri.

Loss and Heartache

"Are you willing to miss their life experiences?" Dr. Kocherhans asked. "More importantly, do you want to miss their lives?" Then he asked the most compelling question: "I would like you to think about that carefully…Devri, do you remember the heartache you felt when your dad died?" Immediately, my heart tensed with a memory tucked tightly away, a topic I had determinedly avoided for years. Every day, I miss my father, who was taken suddenly by a heart attack. I turned slowly to look at Dr. Kocherhans, and I thought to myself, *No, I do not want my family saddened by my loss.*

Something inside of me flipped that day, like a light switch being turned on. For the first time in years, I felt a compelling form of happiness. I knew what I wanted, and it wasn't to die. I wanted to live—but not just live; my desire was to thrive! Something deep within me screamed *You are living…But you could do and be so much more!* That day, I felt the profound nature of what I could become.

This wise therapist gave me an assignment that day. "Go home, and take the time to visualize what you really want out of life. If you could have or be anything, what would it be? What does Devri want out of life? Visualize your successes and achievements, write down your thoughts, and bring them to our next session."

I took this task very seriously. I spent that week contemplating life, and I carefully composed the list, which was a difficult task. During our next visit, Dr. Kocherhans asked me to share the list I had created. As I read, I felt overwhelming sadness. As much as I wished for more, my life didn't add up to much.

Dr. Kocherhans listened patiently to my list, and then he said, "I asked you for a list of what you wanted out of life: your goals and dreams. I looked forward to you sharing with me your desired achievements and success." His head tilted slightly and his voice softened. "However…" He paused and took a breath before continuing. "What I am hearing is a message of loss. You are searching for happiness, you are seeking the affection of your husband, your business is suffering, and you are questioning your parenting."

We took the next several minutes to discuss in detail my experience from the previous week. "Share with me some of the specific thoughts," he said. "Your mind-set as you recorded each item."

The challenges of life had become my all-consuming target. My therapist was right; my mind centered completely on what I didn't have. I couldn't see any good in life—no future, no hope. Then Dr. Kocherhans shared a concept that would forever change the way I focused my thoughts.

"How you think, feel, and act is your choice," he said.

I nodded. "Yes, I know my actions are my choice, but it's hard to control experiences when other people control the situation." I hadn't wanted the divorce, but the final decision to move forward with the divorce had come because of the actions of others.

"What I am saying," he replied, "is that if you allow an unpleasant thought to dwell in your mind long enough, thoughts promote feelings. You can become depressed. Eventually, this feeling will influence how you react to a situation." He sat up in his chair and leaned forward to make a point. "Listen carefully. Your thoughts affect your feelings, and these feelings can influence your actions."

Thinking Makes It So

"Thoughts are just thoughts," Dr. Kocherhans said, "and they are not always based on reality. They are based on our perception of reality, which can at times be deceiving."

Seeing my furrowed brow, he pressed on. "In *Hamlet*, Shakespeare wrote, 'There is nothing either good or bad, but thinking makes it so.' In other words, our thoughts affect how we feel and eventually influence our actions."

He looked directly at me and said, "Devri, the choice is yours. What you allow your thoughts to focus on is what you will get. When you focus on loss, your feelings and actions will support loss."

Dr. Kocherhans looked up and away for a moment, as if thinking. Then he said, "I do not define thoughts as positive or negative, as many in the world believe. I categorize thoughts in two ways: they are either productive or nonproductive. Productive thoughts move you forward toward achieving a goal. Nonproductive thoughts keep you stagnant—in the same place—or moving away from your desired goal." He broke into a smile as he watched me grasping the concept.

"Belief, whether in something tangible or intangible, can build confidence and help you focus on productive thoughts, even when life seems unbearable." He paused for a moment, as if to make a point. "Nonproductive thoughts often trigger fear or feelings of fear associated with events or experiences of the past, which can kill confidence. Belief and fear cannot exist together—meaning, if you change nonproductive thoughts to productive ones, you can have the confidence and ability to change how you feel.

"Devri, it's not easy, but it's simple: learn to focus on productive thoughts, and your experiences in life will improve. Happiness will find you."

This clicked. It felt right. For the first time in ages, I felt hope. As I took another deep breath, I could feel something changing within. *Am I really ready for this?* I asked myself. After years of nonproductive thoughts, despair, and loss, could I really turn it all around?

Buried Deep Within

Dr. Kocherhans seemed to sense my reluctance, and he pressed forward to guide me through it. "We've talked about your divorce, and you shared your feelings of abandonment and disappointment. Do you realize you avoid any discussion about your father's death?"

I nodded, and I immediately felt a stabbing emotional pain. I placed my hand on my heart, trying to contain it, and I slowly exhaled. I had consciously changed the topic many times in the past in order to avoid this discussion. I dreaded the feelings it evoked.

"I think now is an appropriate time to discuss it," Dr. Kocherhans said. "Are you OK with that?"

I didn't particularly want to have this very difficult conversation. My father's death came in the midst of the toughest time of my life—during the first of many marital separations in the final years of my failing marriage. The separation and eventual divorce alone caused so much heartache for my children and me. My father's death during that time seemed unbearable.

Even then, several years later, just thinking about my dad made my heart ache. This time I would be brave. For the first time in my life, no matter how difficult, I would choose to share my feelings about his death.

I took a deep breath and began. "As you know, my dad passed away unexpectedly of a heart attack." As I opened the door on that scary, dark place, the sadness and frustration came billowing out. "I am hurt and a little angry...angry at the Lord for taking him at such a crucial time for me." Fighting back the tears, I felt that uncomfortable squeeze again begin to engulf my heart. I gently tapped my chest with my fingertips and tried to breathe.

"Take your time," Dr. Kocherhans said patiently. "When you are ready, continue."

"I looked to my dad for strength. For encouragement during dark times." The anger began to well up inside of me as I spat out, "He is my dad...I need him in my life, especially now, more than ever!"

The outburst surprised me. I hadn't realized the depth of the fury built up inside. I continued, "How do I get through this life without him?" The grief bubbled over. "I still can't believe he's dead." I sat quietly for a moment, feeling overwhelming sadness, tears welling up and running down my cheeks.

Learning to Recognize

I stared into the distance for a long while. Then Dr. Kocherhans quietly asked, "From what we discussed earlier about productive thinking, share with me the thoughts you have about your father's death, productive or nonproductive."

He handed me a piece of paper and asked me to draw a vertical line to divide the page in half. Then he asked me to write some one-word productive feelings on the right side of the page. I could only think of a few.

Next, he asked me to write one-word nonproductive feelings on the left side of the page. Those came easily; there were many of them. Considering the recent outburst, I wrote *sadness, anger, pain, loss, grief,* and a myriad of other words describing the emotions that had flooded my heart over the years.

When my writing slowed, Dr. Kocherhans asked, "From this exercise, what would you say: productive or nonproductive?"

I looked at the page. "Nonproductive?" I looked at the paper. "Most of the words are on the left side of the page, and they are not helping me to improve. Right?"

"Yes, I would say nonproductive," Dr. Kocherhans said, "because they keep you stuck, focusing on what you have lost. Devri, where are the productive words? *Love, hope, encouragement*...there must be more.

"Over these past seven years, your family has watched your mind and body waste away to the point that you have lost the drive to live. It's not just your medical doctor who's concerned for you. It's your family, me, your friends." His eyes narrowed. "Your doctor specifically told you that if you do not do something different, your health will kill you.

"Years ago, you went to bed, and the depression took over." His gaze narrowed further with understanding.

"I'm not saying life isn't difficult," Dr. Kocherhans said. "I can't even imagine the heartache you've gone through. What's happening, though, is that on a daily basis, you allow your thoughts to focus on the loss of your father, the divorce, and how much both of those experiences hurt.

"My intention is to teach you a way to help you deal with loss. Then you will be able to use these experiences as a way to improve your life.

"What is happening is directly related to your thoughts," he said. "You must learn to let go of nonproductive thoughts by replacing them with productive thoughts. It's about what you focus on." He pointed to his brain. "Your mind-set."

He looked at me and asked, "Devri, what is your *why*? What gets you out of bed each day?"

I thought for a moment but could not think of much.

"When you identify the *why*, you can use it to help you stay motivated through difficult times. From the stories of your father, I believe he is a big part of your *why*. Am I correct?"

"For sure, I want to make my father proud. He was such a good, hardworking, kind man. I would do anything to honor his memory." I paused for a moment to reflect. Dad would have been very disappointed in my actions. "I am not doing a very good job, am I?"

"What you have shared with me about your father, he would never"—he paused to emphasize the word—"*never* want you to suffer like this. Devri, he's not coming back. Your dying will not bring him back."

I Am My Father's Daughter

I sat quietly for a few minutes, struggling to swallow a message I knew to be true. My dad was gone, and for the first time, I realized that no matter how hard I grieved, he would never return, at least not in this life. *I am...my father's daughter,* I thought. *He would never want me to suffer because of his loss.* Yet I realized my thoughts were doing just that. Nonproductive thoughts were affecting my feelings and in turn influencing my actions. I had to make a change, a radical change in what I said to myself in my own mind. I realized that *what you focus on, you believe—and what you believe, you achieve!* I would choose to focus on what I was destined to become! "I am...my father's daughter!" Those words spilled out of my mouth with excitement. They encompassed strength, happiness, love, hope, success, and so much more.

What you focus on you believe,
and what you believe, you achieve!

LightningMoments.com

Dr. Kocherhans looked at me intently, and then we both smiled. As I thought more about productive thinking, my smile broke into a face-wide grin. I felt a Lightning Moment: I knew something within me had changed forever. It could have come from this newfound knowledge about productive thinking, it could have come from lifting the burden from my heart of memories stuffed away for so long, or it could have been both. Whatever happened, happiness finally escaped and filled my entire soul. It felt good. Claiming "who I am" felt good!

I felt the yearning deep within, an inner voice that said, *You are more than you are living. Now just do it!*

"Yes," I said, with joy in my heart, "I am my father's daughter, and I am smart. I can do this. If I focus my mind-set, I can do hard things. I have the skills and talent to accomplish the desires of my heart."

I would claim "who I am" with productive thinking—owning it, allowing these words to define me in a positive, productive way.

Claiming Who "I Am"

In English, the statement is "I am." In French, it's *Je suis*. In German, it's *Ich bin*. In Spanish, it's *Yo soy*. No matter what language you speak, *I* and *am* are still two of the most powerful words when combined. Whatever follows these two words, you have the power to *become*.

Watch what you say within your own mind, because that is what you will become. "I am stupid"—you are right. "I am a loser"—that is correct. "I am lonely, sad, misunderstood, heavy, poor at math, tired, not good enough." If you say it often enough, that is exactly what you will become. You can turn yourself into your worst nightmare.

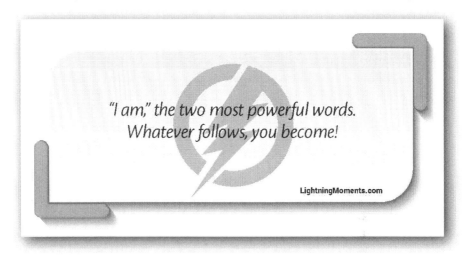

"I am," the two most powerful words.
Whatever follows, you become!

LightningMoments.com

The opposite is also true. "I am beautiful." Yes you are! Inside and out. "I am confident." Absolutely! "I am generous, peaceful, organized, successful, healthy, happy, and courageous." Say it often enough and put a little emotion behind it, and you can become whatever follows these two words. It all starts with productive thought.

Productive Thought and Claiming Who "I Am"—An Activity

Choose a goal, decision, or an experience. Think freely about this topic for several minutes, and then take the time to record the thoughts you had about it—both the productive ones and the nonproductive ones on the "Claiming Who 'I am...!' Productive Thought" Activity sheet in the "Knowledge in Action" section at the end of this chapter. Remember that productive thoughts move you forward toward your goal and happiness.

Chapter 4
Dynamics of Thought
Claiming Who "I am...!"

Knowledge in *Action*

LightningMoments.com

Claiming Who "I am...!"

Complete the Claiming Who "I am" Productive Thought Activity by recording any nonproductive thoughts on the left side of the sheet and productive thoughts on the right side of the page. Ask yourself the following questions: Are my thoughts focused more on productive or nonproductive thinking? What do I need to change to focus on productive thought? Finally, write your own "I am..." statement.

Claiming Who "I am...!" - Productive Thought Activity	
Non-Productive	**Productive**

My Thoughts are:

"I am..." Goal Affirmation
Personal • Present • Productive
The two most powerful words "I am... " Write a simple Affirmation:

CHAPTER 5

Productive Thinking and Affirmation
Focus Your Thoughts; Create Your Reality!

n the therapist's office that day, I began to create my list of goals. This list turned into thirteen goals in all, composed in a five-year plan. As I thought about moving toward achieving these goals, I quickly realized that using productive thinking would be an uphill battle. I was used to wallowing in nonproductive thoughts, and productive thinking would go against my nature. I would need to change the game drastically!

Changing Nonproductive Thought

At one point, my friend Valerie, who is also a therapist, shared with me her observations about my thoughts. I have to say, it stung a little when she agreed with Dr. Kocherhans. She also suggested my thoughts could be affecting my feelings and ruining my happiness. I immediately looked inward and thought, *See, I am bad.*

Valerie recognizing my discouraged look, replied, "It's not you that's bad! Your thinking is negative. Learn to *recognize* your thoughts and *release and replace* the negative ones. Then you will find more happiness."

Valerie was right! Nonproductive thoughts were affecting my feelings and influencing my actions. In other words, nonproductive thoughts *were* running my life, and I alone had the power to change where I placed my focus. By focusing on productive thoughts, I could create my reality. I made a conscious decision to begin *recognizing each nonproductive thought* and then taking steps to release that nonproductive thought by giving myself *permission to release* the thought and finally *replace* the nonproductive thought with a productive thought. My thoughts would be my starting point!

Focus your thoughts; create your reality—either productive or nonproductive. We all face this same challenge. It's up to you (yes, you alone) to change your nonproductive thinking and replace it with productive thoughts. As much as I did not want to admit it, I alone brought negativity into my life by magnifying nonproductive thinking. It had become an obsessive habit; I allowed nonproductive thoughts to rattle around in my brain, and this habit of nonproductive thinking controlled my life.

Focus your thoughts; create your reality!

LightningMoments.com

Let's explore what we can do to change or improve a nonproductive habit. Habits are something we do automatically; very little thought or effort goes into the habit. Try this experiment: Hold your hands out in front of you, elbows straight and palms up. Now, fold your arms. Notice how quickly you performed this action and which arm is on top. Release your arms and hold them in front of you again. Now, fold your arms again, this time placing the opposite arm on top. Did you notice that the action was a little more difficult? Did it feel odd? Why?

You are in the habit of crossing your arms a specific way, with your right or left arm on top. Like most people, you are a creature of habit; with little or no effort, you can fold your arms. In fact, you probably do not even have to think about it as you do it. However, when you try to fold your arms with the opposite arm on top, it's slightly more difficult, and it may feel strange, at least at first. You actually have to think about placing the opposite arm on top as you go through the process. With a little conscious effort, you *can* learn to fold your arms automatically in either direction, without any hesitation or thought. Many therapists use a similar method to assist you in changing nonproductive thinking to a habit of productive thinking. It combines focusing your thought and using affirmations, a common technique in both therapy and professional development. However, when you add the element of "releasing" a nonproductive thought and then replacing that thought—a technique that I learned from my friend Valerie and Dr. Kocherhans, both family therapists—the results can often be substantially more effective in improving behavior.

Cancel-Cancel, Recognize, Release, and Replace

You can change and refocus a thought from nonproductive to productive by using "cancel-cancel, recognize, release, and replace," a technique I dubbed "CC&3Rs" for easy recall.

Mentally stop a nonproductive thought by saying, "Cancel-cancel." Then focus on releasing and finally replacing that thought with a productive thought, feeling, or action. It takes consistency. It's almost impossible to just discard a nonproductive thought—you *must* replace it with something productive; otherwise, there seems to be a void. Changing your thought patterns takes a long-term commitment, but the steps work. Try it!

Using the dialog sequence suggested by Valerie, recognize nonproductive thinking, stop that thought, and then give yourself permission to release the feeling by using the dialog in the following order: "Cancel-cancel...I release the feeling of _____ (the nonproductive thought) and replace it with _____ (add your productive affirmation)." That's it. Focus your thought; create your reality!

Using Affirmations

During the lightning strike, I learned the incredible power of thought firsthand. What seemed like an eternity to me as the lightning racked my body was actually only a split second. Somehow, there was enough time for my brain to experience a series of thoughts and events. Even after the lightning strike took my physical control, I was able to open my eyes simply through the power of my thoughts and visualization.

Like that productive phrase "Open your eyes," affirmations had helped me achieve my goals for years leading up to the lightning strike. In a class I had taken at work eight years prior, I learned that affirmations are positive "I am" statements that, when used consistently, can help you direct your thoughts to take action. Affirmations include three components: they must be personal, present, and positive (what I call productive).

- **Personal:** The affirmation is about you. Use *I* or your name.
- **Present:** Apply present-tense words such as *am*. Avoid using terms focused on the future tense, such as *I will* or *I want to*.
- **Productive:** Link your affirmation to your goal with productive words, especially its result (happy, successful, etc.). Visualization is key!

To write my own personal affirmation, I began with my most controlling nonproductive thought: "My dad is dead. My life will never be happy without him."

First, I had to *recognize* it as a nonproductive thought. Next, I *released* it, saying, "Cancel-cancel. I release the feelings of loss and missing my dad." Finally, I tweaked and *replaced* it with a productive thought: "My dad is watching over me. He loves me and wants me to live a happy life!"

Then I took this further to become a personal, present, productive affirmation. "I am my father's daughter. I am happy and successful at everything I do!" I could finally visualize myself as happy, successful, and using my dad's memory productively.

Consistency Is the Key

Using the cancel-cancel, recognize, release, and replace system, I created several affirmations that supported my goals to assist in overcoming the nonproductive thoughts. However, as much as I tried to use the affirmations, the nonproductive thoughts kept returning; in fact, they seemed to be increasing in number and strength. I realized that I had a chronic case of nonproductive thinking. I had become that constantly negative individual whose life centered around what was not working and what I had lost. Stress and challenges followed my every move. It seemed as if a little black cloud followed me around. If something was going to go wrong, it usually happened to me! As soon as I changed one nonproductive thought, another one crept into my mind. I felt like the person whom others dread being around.

I realized using an affirmation once or twice a day is not enough to refocus a nonproductive thought pattern. To overcome habitual nonproductive thinking, like crossing your arms a specific way, I had to consciously do something different over and over. I began to use CC&3Rs and affirmations for everything. I added to my CC&3Rs by carrying cards with my affirmations and goals written on them. I placed these cards on my bathroom mirror, on my car visors, by the kitchen sink, on my bedroom door, and on my front door to remind me to do my CC&3Rs. Twenty to fifty times a day, if needed, I would repeat the phrase "cancel-cancel" and then replace the thought with a productive affirmation. Yes, it took a constant effort to recognize, release, and replace nonproductive thoughts, but the results were worth it. Within a few short months of consistent effort, my life began to change.

Write Your Own Productive Affirmation

Let's go through an example of a productive affirmation using the CC&3Rs technique. Suppose the thought "I am not good enough" comes into your mind, train yourself to immediately say, "Cancel-cancel! I release the feeling that I am not good enough, and I replace this thought with 'I am successful and an inspiration to others!'" Now visualize yourself *living* the new thought; visualize a successful life and others coming to you for advice.

Quick Review—CC&3Rs

- **Cancel-cancel:** Stop the nonproductive thought in its tracks.
- **Recognize:** Ask yourself what you really want, and identify nonproductive versus productive thoughts.
- **Release:** Let go of the nonproductive thought. "I give myself permission to release the feeling of _____."
- **Replace:** Immediately substitute with a productive thought or positive affirmation that aligns with your goals.
- Visualize yourself living your positive affirmation.

You, too, can develop the habit of overcoming nonproductive thinking and move one step closer to living the life of your dreams. Over months (well, actually, years), I have consistently used the CC&3Rs technique to develop the skill to quickly recognize nonproductive thinking, release those thoughts, and replace them with productive thoughts that move me closer to my goals. It has not always been easy. I often find myself needing to use cancel-cancel many times a day; however, the extra effort to control nonproductive thoughts is worth every ounce of energy. Using affirmations is hands down the number-one skill that helped me learn to control my thoughts, get out of bed, and begin living life again. I now enjoy the new habit I created: productive thinking!

You might be saying to yourself, "Yeah, sure, positive thinking is great. But I've been positive before, and it hasn't worked! I've lost weight and gained it back again. I've tried to quit smoking more times than I can count. And I've had plenty of days where I did not want to get out of bed." You're absolutely right! Believe me, as I struggled in the aftermath of my dad's death and the divorce, I felt that way too—until I realized that understanding the importance of positive thought is only the first step to correcting nonproductive thinking. The next crucial step is discovering your purpose for achieving a goal. In chapter 6, I will share with you how to achieve goals more quickly and more successfully by connecting with the *why* behind your goal.

Use the "CC&3Rs—Cancel-Cancel, Recognize, Release, and Replace" activity sheet in the "Knowledge in Action" section at the end of this chapter to write your own CC&3Rs.

Chapter 5
Productive Thinking and Affirmations
Focus Thought, Create Your Reality!

Knowledge in *Action*

LightningMoments.com

Productive Thinking and Affirmations

Write your own – CC&3R's and then perform the activity to recognize, release and replace nonproductive thinking.

CC&3R's – Cancel, Cancel: Recognize, Release and Replace	
CANCEL, CANCEL	Stop the nonproductive and ask: "What is it that I want?" Write the thought below:
RECOGNIZE	"Will this current desire help me to achieve my goal?" Write your discoveries below:
RELEASE	"I give myself permission to release _____." Record the thoughts or actions you need to release here:
REPLACE	"I will replace it with _____." Describe productive thoughts and actions here:
NOTES:	Record any additional feelings/thoughts:

CHAPTER 6

Connecting Your Goal with "Why?"

Getting below the Surface

"How did it feel?" This was the question people most frequently asked me following the lightning strike. The details of this rare experience breed curiosity. Yet because the actual strike encompassed such a small fraction of the entire ordeal, the question I feel a lightning-strike survivor *should* be asked is "How did it feel *after* the strike?" The painful recovery is much longer than the actual split-second event, and it includes both a physical and an emotional roller coaster. Most important, healing from a lightning strike does not come with a "what to expect" handbook.

The Art of Connecting the *Why*

Focusing on loss is a vicious cycle. I had lost both physical and mental skills because of the lightning strike. My thoughts affected my feelings, and my feelings influenced my unwanted actions. But I simply could not get out of the rut! This thought—*you are never going to get better*—prompted nonproductive feelings. The overwhelming sadness resulted in a physical reaction: crying. I stayed in bed most of the day. Changing my focus to productive thought would break the vicious cycle, at least for a little while, but over time, the thoughts would return. I was stuck! There must be more to it than just changing a thought! As much as I used the CC&3Rs with actualization—affirmations and visualizations—these activities alone were not enough. To get unstuck, I needed more. I needed willpower, drive, and strength.

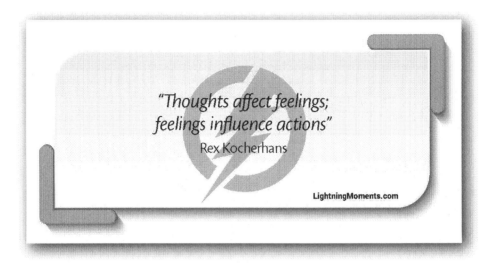

"Thoughts affect feelings;
feelings influence actions"
Rex Kocherhans

LightningMoments.com

Often mistaken for willpower, connecting with *why* is much more than just "sheer will." Linking your goals to productive thought will promote productive feelings. However, if you link your goal to productive thought *and* a powerful emotional connection, the entire process becomes more effective—and likely permanent. It's an art, connecting your goals with your *why*. The opposite is also true: link a nonproductive thought to an emotional connection, and it will produce a much stronger nonproductive reaction.

One particularly mortifying night, it clicked for me. I awoke from a deep sleep with a nagging rumble in my gut. I had to get to the bathroom and get there fast! With the paralysis, my legs wouldn't carry me, and I couldn't make it alone. In desperation, I quietly called my husband, who was sound asleep behind me. "Don?"

Knowing I could not roll over due to pain and limited mobility and not wanting to cause me additional pain by leaning over my body, Don quickly jumped up, ran around the bed, and placed his face in front of mine. "What do you need, sweetheart?"

"I have to get to the bathroom...right now," I cried.

Without hesitation, my wonderful husband scooped me into his arms and carried me the twenty steps. As he lowered me onto the commode, the diarrhea poured from my body. I was horrified. In four years of marriage, he had never seen me even sit on the toilet, let alone go to the bathroom. This was an action I never intended to share. Yet here I sat, unable to control my bowels and absolutely mortified. Tears filled my eyes and began to run down my cheeks.

Don softly wiped away the tears. "Sweetheart, what's wrong? What is upsetting you?"

"I never wanted you to see me like this," I sobbed.

Don knelt in front of me and held me gently in his arms. "Oh, sweetheart, it's OK. I love you," he said.

Fear welled within my body—but why? It felt vaguely familiar. Then the memory of a final struggle scrolled within my mind, and I let it play out. Within weeks of her cancer's return, Lauri became wheelchair bound, the disease quickly weakening her spine. And then, almost as suddenly as the final bout began, she was gone.

Identifying the *Why*

This memory of Lauri triggered that emotional connection with my goal. Now, seven years later, there I sat with my husband, unable to control my legs. We had avoided a disaster, at least this time. Though this experience of losing control of my bowels in front of Don was upsetting, through my memory of Lauri's struggles, I had discovered the *why* behind my goal. Instead of focusing on what I did not have or what I couldn't do, I had discovered the *purpose* of my goal: I wanted to walk unassisted again, of course, but what I really wanted was to take care of my family, not the other way around. Although I knew Don would lovingly care for me the rest of my life, I also knew that if I put forth the effort—and it would take a huge amount of effort—I could regain the use of my body. This *why*, the desire for independence, became the emotional connection to my goal. Some people use the word *willpower*—that determination to keep going when times get tough. Tie this into your thoughts, using CC&3Rs, and your goal becomes reality.

Although movement was extremely agonizing, I knew that with enough concentration on specific muscles, I could move. The alternative—avoiding the pain by choosing not to move—could result in never regaining full use of my limbs. I had watched Lauri's body wither so quickly, and now I could feel my own limbs losing their mass through lack of use. Pushing through the pins and needles of exercise, I visualized Lauri on the sidelines, cheering me on with each step. Even years after her passing, Lauri is still an example to me. To the very end, she never gave up, and neither would I.

Learning the Art of Goal Setting

In the fourth grade, I discovered a love for setting goals, and I began to set goals for everything. In my teens, I actually wrote a goal-setting system—many of the aspects of that system are included in this book. Over the years, as I periodically reviewed my goals, I noticed a pattern. The list of accomplished goals grew with new additions, but there were goals on my list that, month after month, year after year, went unachieved. That puzzled me. Why was I able to achieve so many goals, yet a simple few seemed to remain outside my reach? I've noticed the same pattern with other individuals.

I began to question the process. People set goals all the time, but what keeps them from achieving their goals? The answer is the importance of the *why* behind a goal. I did not achieve goals that I had not connected with emotionally, because the *why* remained undefined. Let's discuss this emotional connection that can help you keep going when you are ready to give up. Recall that the first step in goal setting is to identify *what* you want to accomplish. I believe that the moment you set a goal, you take the first step toward victory. You attract into your life whatever you focus on, so once you identify the *what* and write it down, the powers in the universe kick into action to assist you in achieving this goal. It's frequently called the power of attraction; I believe this power to be spiritual strength. Through faith, you attract into your life whatever you give your focus.

The "Stuff"

"What you think about, you bring about." Ponder that phrase for a moment. If it were that easy, we would all be achieving our goals, right? Well, we are not. Why? There's another layer to the cake. First, we must explore the "stuff" (the negative baggage, undealt-with emotions, or heartache that we try to hide or avoid instead of dealing with). This stuff is stored within our minds or bodies. It's like clutter that can get in the way and can keep us from achieving our goal.

Let me share an example of emotional clutter that I allowed to affect my life. I left high school halfway through my junior year; I was sixteen years old and pregnant. Five days later, I married my first husband and prepared to take on the responsibilities of motherhood. For many years, I quietly carried the personal embarrassment of my sudden departure from high school; I stuffed the experience inside and refused to talk about it, instead focusing every effort on being a perfect wife and mother.

Over the years, I often avoided contact with former friends and classmates, feeling that "I wasn't good enough." A decade later, my good friend Lauri—one of the only high-school friends with whom I had maintained contact—convinced me to attend our ten-year high-school reunion with her. I agreed. That evening, however, I was filled with horrific pangs of inadequacy as I compared myself to each classmate who seemed secure and successful—everything I lacked. After that event, I vowed never to place myself in that awkward situation again.

Fast-forward twenty years. Life had changed dramatically; I actually looked forward to attending my thirty-year high-school reunion and sharing life's triumphs with friends I had long missed. I had a successful career and a family, and most importantly, I was happily married to Don. I left the event that evening feeling happy. I remember walking to the car, stopping my sweet husband right in the parking lot, and saying, "Thank you for being here with me, and thank you for *loving* me." Life felt fantastic!

What had made the difference in my attitude between the ten-year reunion and the thirty-year reunion? It was the stuff—those thoughts and events I had kept hidden or stuffed below the surface. At the time of the ten-year reunion, I had been married for more than eleven years. I had finished high school with honors at a private school. I was happily raising four beautiful children, my then-husband and I owned our own home, and I owned my own salon. Yet all of this success paled in comparison to the humiliation I felt about dropping out of high school while pregnant. I could not enjoy my present achievements because of past events I perceived as failures. These experiences I kept hidden below the surface were unknowingly influencing my current feelings and, in turn, my actions.

So, how do you keep the stuff from affecting your current situation negatively?

Think of it this way. On the surface, there are experiences that others see easily, such as our achievements, our work, and our family involvement—the life we are currently living. Then there are things below the surface. These experiences are at times a little harder to see, such as childhood hurts or events and family or relationship dynamics. It's important to note that not all experiences stored below the surface, these background experiences, are nonproductive; some are productive. Each experience in life fills your "box"—a.k.a. your comfort zone—and can help you to become a successful individual. (We will learn more about your box, and how to expand it, in chapter 7.) Experiences from life, whether productive or nonproductive, subconsciously affect your current actions. Though you may try to quietly tuck them away, your experiences can affect how you feel and react to things in the present. If we do not forgive and let go, these past events can affect our current situation, no matter how hard we try to ignore or stuff them.

This below-the-surface background stuff can get in the way of your current goals, possibly preventing you from ever achieving them. When asked correctly, questions will help you get below the surface; they will help you identify past feelings, actual events, or experiences and connect you with the emotions that can help you achieve your goal. This emotional connection will help you, when life gets difficult, to stay motivated by reminding you of why it is important for you to achieve your goal.

The Emotional Aspect

The emotional aspect of a goal is what drives you to keep going when life gets in the way. It does not matter how defined a goal is or how much action you put into achieving it. If you are not emotionally connected to the goal, achieving it or maintaining it can be difficult. You create this emotional connection by identifying what you want to achieve and then asking questions—beginning with *why* you want to achieve a particular goal. Discover the underlying feeling that you will experience when you achieve it. Emotions are *huge* motivators that can help move you toward goal achievement. An emotional aspect can help you stay committed.

Take, for example, the number-one New Year's resolution: "I want to lose weight." It's easy to place it at the top of your goal list. If you put it on your list and stop there, you are setting yourself up for failure. Once the goal is set, it's important to examine *what* is driving you toward goal achievement. To dig below the surface and identify the goal's emotional connection, apply the question technique. Here's an example:

What do you want to achieve?
I want to lose weight.

Why is this goal important to you?
I want to look and feel better.

Again...Why is looking or feeling better important to you?
I am tired all the time. I want to be able to do the things I want to do.

OK...What will be the benefit when you lose weight?
I'll look better and feel better, and I won't age as quickly. I can have a stronger, healthier body.

Dig a little deeper...Why is a healthy body important to you?
Well, I want to be able to participate in activities with my grandkids. I want to be a fun grandma like my grandmother was.

OK...We are getting somewhere. Why is being a fun grandma vital? What are you feeling right now?

My grandmother was amazing. I loved playing with her. But then it seemed as if one day when I was very young, the playing stopped—she would have been in her early fifties. She began sitting in her chair and reading her books. She didn't come out and play with us anymore. It made me sad. I do not think it was because she was sick in any way, because she seemed to go out with the adults when she wanted to. It just seemed as if her books became more important. I kind of felt left out.

So what is your plan of action? What do you think you need to do next?
I am going to keep moving. I loved it when my grandma played outside with us in the gutters as it rained; it was fun cooking all day in the kitchen to prepare for a huge family dinner or fun snacks. We laughed, worked, and played hard. Then it seemed as if on one visit to her home, it stopped. I did not know why. I want to always be that fun grandma, and I believe involvement and activity will help to keep my mind and body strong.

Great, now we are below the surface. Finally, let's dig a little deeper by asking, "Is there anything we've missed?" Listen for any other emotions or feelings that may come to light.
Now that I am older, I do believe lack of movement—sitting in her chair—slowed her down. I really missed the fun times of playing with my grandma. I kind of feel as if I lost a lot of years. I want to be there for my grandkids; I want to be an important part of their lives.

Why does this affect you so much?
You know, I just realized…My goal isn't about losing weight. It's about health and energy. I want to maintain strength into my senior years. I want to be able to make fun memories with my grandkids. Live life without getting tired. Most of all, I want to be remembered as a fun grandma.

There you go…Using the question technique, we were able to dig below the surface. We discovered an experience (missed fun with grandma)—the emotional connection—that can motivate healthy living and help us maintain the desire for a strong and energetic body into our senior years. The benefit will be memories built with family.

Details Come from Digging

In the previous example, each time we asked questions, additional details were identified. Using the question technique to dig below the surface of a goal can identify specific information and an emotional connection to your goal. The deeper you dig, the more detailed and specific the answers become. Continue asking the question and feeling the emotion until you get to the root of the *why*. Then ask, "Is there anything we've missed?" Listen for the answer. Write down any additional items that come up during this activity. Discover the emotional connection to your goal, and you will have the drive to achieve!

Discovering Your *Why*

Now, take the time necessary to discover the *why* behind your desired goal and create an emotional connection. Remember the goal you chose in chapter 3, "Action Plan." Write your identified goal in the "Why?" question activity provided in the "Knowledge in Action" section at the end of this chapter. Use the question technique to identify the emotional connection with your goal by writing your answers in the page provided. Be honest with yourself and keep asking "who, what, why, when, and how" questions even when it gets emotionally difficult to answer. Record your thoughts and feelings to support your goal achievement.

Releasing the Below-the-Surface Stuff

The big mystery to goal achievement is the bundle of experiences hidden below the surface. Until I began this question activity, I thought my departure-from-high-school experience was neatly tucked away. What event is waiting for you to dig up and release through affirmations? Once you have identified your goal and used the question technique to discover the stuff below the surface, use the CC&3Rs to recognize, release, and replace any nonproductive feelings with productive thought. You may need to perform the CC&3Rs many times over a period of weeks or months to release and replace the thought or experience that has been buried for so long.

The Goal Affirmation

The next step is to write a goal affirmation from the answers you gleaned in the "Why?" questioning activity you will find in the "Knowledge in Action" section at the end of this chapter. We have already talked about affirmations needing to be personal, productive, and present. This affirmation technique will help you stay focused when life gets in the way. Here's an affirmation that could come from the answers in the question technique applied above:

> I am a happy, supportive grandmother; my life is fun and fulfilling! I weigh _____ pounds, the perfect weight for me. I exercise each day and choose healthy foods. I look and feel fabulous. I have unlimited energy to play with the grandkids. We make incredible memories. I am a fun grandma!

Take a few minutes to write your goal affirmation using the following system:

1. Clearly identify your goal.
2. Write the goal in the present tense, using "I am" or "I, (your name), am."
3. Use productive "linking" adjectives—such as *successful, happy, loving*—that combine your desired goals with emotions.
4. Clearly state the impact that the goal achievement will have in your life.
5. Write a simple affirmation that includes your goal and the *why*.

Visualization Activity

Now that you know how to write a goal affirmation, take the time to visualize yourself achieving your goal by creating a mental picture and repeating the affirmation. Find a comfortable place to relax, and silence your cell phone. Create a place of balance within your mind and body by releasing any nonproductive thoughts or stress and focusing on peace. Within your mind, begin by walking yourself visually through each step; see yourself successfully achieve your goal. Live the experience in the first person. Enjoy each accomplishment using your senses: how it feels; what you see; and what you smell, taste, or hear. Focus consistently on feeling the emotional excitement of having already achieved your goal.

Additional Tips for Successful Goal Achievement

- Create a dream board with photos, or create a smaller version by writing your goal affirmation on a three-by-five card or on the back of a photo. Look at the card frequently.
- Focus on this board or goal card several times a day.

- Connect to your goal emotionally by using the question technique to get below the surface and uncover the stuff. Then use CC&3Rs to recognize, release, and replace any nonproductive feeling with productive thought.
- As you visualize your goal, play a song or music with a great motivational message or an instrumental piece with a great beat. Music can enhance the body's energy and increase balance.
- Repeat your goal objective and affirmations as you visualize yourself successfully achieving your goal.
- Every half hour, take two minutes to repeat your affirmation while visualizing the desired outcome.
- When your thoughts get off track, use your CC&3Rs and repeat the affirmation.
- Finally, affirm and visualize your desired outcome.
- Then do it again—repetition is success!

Success in goal achievement will increase as you use the question technique to identify your *why* and create a stronger emotional connection to your goal. Visualizing Lauri on the sidelines cheering me on became my emotional connection to the goal of regaining control of my body. Her example is my inspiration, and honoring her memory through my work became the motivation. To this day, I carry a picture of Lauri with me wherever I go. Now, it's time to connect with your goal by discovering your *why*.

Chapter 6
Connecting your Goal with "WHY?"
Getting Below the Surface

Knowledge in *Action*

LightningMoments.com

Getting Below the Surface

Record your goal in the space provided, and then ask the question: "Why do I want to achieve this goal?" Keep asking what, who, when and why questions until you identify your goal's purpose. Finally write an "I am..." goal affirmation. Anything that follows the two most powerful words "I am..." you have the ability to become. Repeat the "I am..." affirmation several times a day.

"Why?" Question Technique
What is your goal? Write it down.
Ask "Why?"
Keep asking a variety of questions, until you get below the surface.
Ask, "Is there anything we've missed?" and listen for the answer.

"I am..." Goal Affirmation
Personal • Present • Productive
The two most powerful words "I am... " Write a simple affirmation that reflects your goal:

CHAPTER 7

The Box, a.k.a. Your Comfort Zone
Dare to Step Outside of Your Box

For months after the lightning strike, as my body healed, Don and I walked the roads around our home. We discovered early on in my recovery that I was dealing not only with physical challenges but also with emotional ones—specifically, fear. Opening the front door for the first time and leaving the safety of our home became one of the biggest challenges to overcome. I placed my hands on the handle of the walker, took a deep breath, released the air slowly with a big sigh, and said, "OK... let's go."

The fear tightened within my chest as we exited the front door. It took effort to consciously tuck away the threatening tears and muster every ounce of resolution. "Come on," I said out loud, hoping the words would act as an affirmation. "We can do this."

Though I heard the words come from my mouth, I felt billows of fear from deep within, drowning any comfort. My strongest leg, the left, seemed to throw off my balance, as the right leg lagged behind, totally out of tandem. I focused on lifting my right knee and then strategically placing the next step. Slowly, we progressed to the end of the garage and then back to the safety of the front porch.

Our excursion that day was about fifty steps in all—a huge accomplishment. I collapsed onto the bench on the front porch and breathed a sigh of relief. "Yes! I did it!" My legs ached and burned, hot to the touch. Don rubbed them back and forth. The gentle movement felt good, soothing the pain and increasing the circulation.

The next few outings, though still difficult, were not as traumatic. Each time I exited the front door, it seemed to get easier. Over a time, we were able to make it to the end of the driveway—including its slope—and back to the porch. Though walking helped to strengthen and heal my legs, it ignited a dull ache that could last for several hours. To ease the pain, Don would rub my legs after each walk and then help me into a warm bath.

Over time, I progressed to using a cane and walking to the mailbox. As my vigor increased, I eventually made it to the first corner at the end of the street and then the second corner. With only the cane as support at this point, I knew that if I tired, I would need to wait on the neighbor's lawn until Don could run and get the car to drive me home. Being alone, even for a few minutes, would be unthinkable misery. It took months of work, but the day we turned the corner to make that final stretch of the one-mile circle around our complex, we both cheered aloud in triumph.

Once I could walk the neighborhood, we moved to the next stretch of the journey: to speed-walk one leg of the block and then jog the next. Again, jogging increased the painful nerve ache in the muscle and bone above the knee and down the calf. I couldn't wait to get home, knowing a warm bath with essential oils and a firm massage for my legs were awaiting me. Next came a slow, short jog, and then came a bigger challenge: balancing a bike. Even though the speed was slow, it felt exhilarating. After months of visualizing the bike ride, I felt the muscles flex as my legs pumped the pedals. "Yes! I am riding my bike!" It was a simple ride up the street and back to the garage, yet an Olympic triumph for me.

Over a few weeks, Don and I rode our bikes around the safety of our quiet neighborhood streets. Then came the next huge challenge: our first biking adventure outside the gated community since the lightning strike. Victory would be mine! I had waited five long months for this. Excited and maybe a little apprehensive, I buckled my helmet. The sun was shining, warming the Las Vegas winter afternoon—a perfect day for a bike ride. I smiled. "I'm ready. Let's go." Don gave me an excited grin and lunged forward as his bike took off down the driveway. I was right behind him.

It felt amazing to push the pedals, one after the other. I couldn't believe I was riding my bike, and in just five months! It felt freeing. After a brief ride through the neighborhood, we reached the farthest point I had accomplished, and we left the safety of our gated community. The gate closed behind us as we made a right turn onto the main street that would take us up the small hill.

Don motioned for me to take the lead. Pedaling became a little harder, and I felt the tension build in my legs. "Come on," I said to myself out loud and then lifted up off the seat to help with the pedaling. One, two, three, four. I counted as I pushed each pedal and pulled the handlebars to give myself more thrust. Shifting to a lower gear seemed to help. The burn in the muscles of my legs remained constant. *You can do this. We are almost to the corner*, I encouraged myself internally. *Then it's downhill for a while. Keep going.* The corner was a welcome sight and represented one leg of this victory.

We picked up speed as we descended the small grade. I enjoyed the break and the gentle flush of wind against my skin. Suddenly, a car whooshed to the side of me. I tightened my grip on the handlebars, which then began to wobble. The bike was out of control. I drifted to the right toward the curb, overcorrected into the lane of traffic, and quickly turned the handlebars again for safety as I pulled the brakes and came to a jolting stop. My chest slammed into the handlebars, and I nearly toppled over the front of the bike. Don, following close behind, barely missed running into the back of my bike. He skimmed past on the left side.

"What happened? Are you OK?" he asked.

"The car passed me, and I freaked out." Tears welled in my eyes; my heart was pounding. My shin ached, and I could see droplets of blood. It was beginning to bruise where I had slammed it on the pedal.

"It's OK," he reassured me. "Are you going to be OK?"

I shook my head to clear my thoughts and took a deep breath, trying to calm my racing heart.

"Here, let me take the lead for a while. We will take it slower." I could hear the concern in Don's voice. He shortened our planned ride, making the big loop around our community and heading home. Following Don seemed easier than taking the lead.

I had set the goal to ride my bike and had worked hard for five months to regain the strength and control of my legs, only to discover my mind couldn't deal with the stress of traffic. My body was ready, but my mind was not. I arrived home from that short ride, exhausted; went right into my room; and crawled into bed. Again, I began to cry as doubt began to creep in. *Do you really think you can overcome a lightning strike?* I asked myself as thoughts of past failures and missed opportunities slipped into my mind. *You failed in the past, and you will continue to fail.* I pulled the sheets over my head and burrowed beneath them, defeated by fear. *I will just stay within the walls of the gated community to ride my bike. I am safe here.*

It seemed life simply would not cooperate. My emotions were like a roller-coaster ride—reaching thrilling highs as I achieved a goal, only to be thrust to the ground with more disappointment.

The Box

At times, obstacles in life just seem too difficult to face. I felt safe in my bedroom, tucked away in bed. Within my domain, I had control. No one could come in or out of my bedroom without my permission. Life was simple—this was my box.

Each of us has a comfort zone. My friend Valerie taught me to visualize a box to reflect the mental boundary or personal space I created around my physical body.

Picture it like this: Hold your hand out as if to indicate "Stop." Now visualize an invisible field—let's say a square box—around your body, about an arm's length in each direction. Visualize a top, a bottom, and all four sides of your box. You maintain this virtual space (the box) by allowing others to enter *or* by physically keeping them out. Having someone enter your virtual box without being invited promotes feelings of discomfort. To regain a feeling of comfort, you slowly take a step (or two) backward to reestablish the invisible boundary you set around your space. The area that the other person entered is your comfort zone. Though the size of the box may differ, each of us has created a mental boundary around our physical body.

Your box can also be composed of mental conditioning or boundaries you have established. This can include specific actions, such as waiting for people to speak to you before you speak to them or choosing not to speak in a public setting or in front of a crowd. No matter how limiting the boundaries may seem, each of us maintains a sense of security by staying within these physical actions or mental behavior. The key to achieving success in this life is to take a step outside of your comfort zone and perform actions that make you feel uncomfortable.

The Stuff in Your Box

The contents of the box are different for each of us. Your box is filled with personal experiences, the culture in which you live (family, work, community), and your personal values or beliefs. Each life event is filtered through this personal box, and you assign meaning to each event based on the items already contained there. Remember when we discussed above-the-surface stuff and below-the-surface stuff? The below-the-surface stuff contributes to your box as well. Often, the stored experiences are productive, but nonproductive stuff can also be stored below. You may have tried to forget these nonproductive experiences or events, but they can still affect how you feel or react to events in the present. For an event that is affecting you nonproductively, it's important to use CC&3Rs in order to let go of past feelings associated with the event or experience.

It's All about Perception

Have you ever wondered why the exact same event produces different versions of the experience for each person involved? Individuals decipher the meaning of an event as it passes through their boxes, filled with personal experiences, culture, values, and beliefs. What emerges at the other end of the box is each person's version of the experience. Often, individuals who experienced the exact same event reach entirely different meanings. For example, many years ago, my sisters and I got together at my home for a few days of family fun. Each sister brought her children; at the time, that added up to eleven cousins in all. After the visit, I received a card from each sister. One card expressed gratitude for the visit and shared memories that would last a lifetime. The other focused on a few specific instances where the cousins had not gotten along, as often happens with most children. I honestly wondered if the three of us had attended the same family get-together, as the messages were so opposite—two completely different "stories" of the same experience. In retrospect, one of my sisters has always loved getting together with family and feels very comfortable in large family situations. The other sister prefers small groups or activities with her immediate family. It makes sense that the larger family situation would make the second sister feel *out of her box*, which could lead her to feel uncomfortable and to take offense easily.

My Home, My Box

In the early months of my recovery from the lightning strike, I created a comfort zone within my home. Movement was difficult at best. At home, I was protected; I chose who could come in and how I would move around. We set up chairs along the walls, and I could reach for a chair to help me get from the bedroom to the kitchen and living room. I could always see the next chair. I set small goals, reaching one chair at a time. I knew I could rest on each chair along the way, for as long as I needed, before moving on to the next goal. I felt safe. To leave the safety of my home meant I had to leave this comfort zone; to do that brought with it crippling fear and anxiety.

My first trips outside home were in a wheelchair. Although it was easier for me to rely on others to push me, many venues are just not made for accessibility or ease of use in a wheelchair. I did not like sitting in a chair all day, and I knew that sitting would not strengthen my body. Another worry included finding a family-accessible bathroom. It was still difficult for me to go to the restroom on my own.

Once I could walk for longer distances, though my steps were slow and labored, we could leave the wheelchair at home. But with this increased freedom came the worry of finding a place to rest along the way, because I tired easily. Needless to say, leaving home meant taking a huge step out of my comfort zone. Whether I was in the wheelchair or walking clumsily, everywhere I went people gave me awkward stares. Although strangers were gracious, I felt like an actor on a stage. It seemed as if people were watching, looking at me differently. When I looked at others, they often looked away. That rarely happened before the strike. This experience felt strangely familiar and brought back a memory from my childhood, an experience hidden within my box, and it was not comfortable.

Let me take a moment to explore this experience stored in my box—and its influence on current events.

Childhood Experience

My father spent much of my childhood in the military, so during those years, my family moved many times. As my family arrived at each new location, the school official would introduce each of us to our new class, which was filled with students who were already comfortable with each other. I remember one class introduction vividly. After living out of the county for several years, my family moved back to the United States. Looking back, I now understand that I had been living in a foreign country with its own culture for nearly three years, and my characteristics were different from those of the typical American. That day I wore a dress we had purchased in Germany. It, too, looked different from what the other students wore. The navy-blue dress was in a dirndl style, with white, puffy sleeves and a hand-stitched apron. I specifically remember one girl in the front row staring at me; she began at my head, and her brows lifted as her eyes moved down to my toes. Her gaze seemed abnormally odd, and I felt out of place.

The students in the class did not immediately accept me; in fact, it was weeks before I made my first real friend. Being shy, I ate lunch by myself each day and often sat on the curb by the blacktop to watch the other students play games during recess. I was only eight at the time, and this experience felt traumatically uncomfortable. I buried the memory deep within my box and interpreted it as meaning that I was "not good enough."

Now, many years later, recovering from the lightning strike, being in a wheelchair or walking laboriously drew stares. These stares filtered through the childhood experiences stored within my box and brought back the sensation of feeling "not good enough." Without actually thinking about it, I had called up the familiar feelings of embarrassment I experienced during the fearful classroom introduction. To avoid feeling not good enough, I sheltered myself inside my home. I realized that with this limited reaction, I could improve my physical skill or health to only a certain point. Although I took actions of visualizing the bike ride, bed standing, and setting goals to walk from chair to chair, these alone would not get the results needed to recover. I needed to work harder. But I was held back by fear based on that childhood event. I knew that if I was going to heal, I needed to release and replace this fear.

Take a Step Outside of Your Box

Now, this takes me back to the nearly catastrophic bike ride outside of the gated community. I returned from the ride and unconsciously sought comfort through past behavior: I climbed into bed and again began to cry.

Don entered the room, took me in his arms, and caressed my hair. "Sweetheart," he said tenderly, "over the past five months, we have enjoyed so many incredible experiences." He dropped his eyes. "I cannot even explain the dreadful worry I felt in the beginning. You would ask me the same question over and over. I remember the exhilarating joy I felt, after the lightning strike, when your thoughts finally began to reconnect." A smile crossed his face.

"Do you remember those first days, when I fed you with a spoon? How we cheered the first time you were able to get a spoonful of cereal to your mouth by yourself? We celebrated the day you moved from the wheelchair to the walker? Remember the work it took to walk to the end of the driveway and back? Your legs would ache so badly, but you did it again the next day because you knew it was going to get you where you wanted to be.

"Now I have a suggestion, if you are game." I recognized Don's sneaky, one-sided smile. He had a plan, and he was excited.

"Go ahead; I'm listening," I muttered through the tears.

"Crawling back into bed is not going to get you what you want." He paused. "The solution is simple: We will load the bikes on the truck and take them to a less busy area for our ride. Somewhere where cars will not be able to bother us."

Kick Yourself into Gear—Move!

Life felt dark and dismal with no peace of mind; I was depressed. I had overcome depression long ago, but at that moment, I could not remember how. Although my current situation—being struck by lightning—was completely different from the divorce or an experience in elementary school, the rejection felt the same, and I reacted the same way. When life's challenges seemed too burdensome, I easily succumbed to defeat and crawled back into bed. Don was right; this behavior would not help me achieve my goals. However, throughout my life, when challenges arose, I stayed within my box by reverting to past reactions—crawling back into bed to hide from the trials. I had to do something different this time.

I realized that with Don's help, I had achieved months of healing from the lightning strike, work that included more physical pain than I could ever imagine putting myself through. But thankfully, despite the pain, we had something to celebrate; we enjoyed mountains of success as healing took place slowly but surely. I continually felt launched out of my comfort zone as every step of the journey brought new challenges. The importance of taking responsibility for each action became clear, and it would play into my being able to let go of past failures that kept getting in the way of healing. I visualized the shy little school girl in the navy-blue dirndl dress; she was beautiful and a fighter. I still have that dress, which my daughter wore to school with pride and joy when she was young.

I resolved to get out of bed and recommit to doing whatever it would take to ride, even if that meant stepping outside of my comfort zone. Having overcome loss in the past, I knew I already possessed what I needed to succeed. I just had to do it!

Emotion Sparks Action

The talk with Don started an emotional chain reaction: I couldn't wait to get back on my bike and ride. Don helped me rediscover my *why*. I realized that when inspiration is sparked by emotion, it promotes motivation—a commitment to action—and can assist in achieving goals. As we analyzed my past ways of coping with challenges and feelings of loss, this event reminded me of a system I had created years before: a tool to kick myself into gear when I needed that little extra jump-start.

Years earlier, Dr. Kocherhans had told me I needed to expand my comfort zone. He said, "The shortest, most reliable way to change how you feel is to change what you are doing." People often limit themselves by what they do. He suggested that depression can be a result of inactivity, and he said I needed to get out of bed and do something.

This was easier said than done, as I had no energy and no motivation. After that specific session with Dr. Kocherhans, I began to study depression in depth, and I

"The shortest most reliable way to change how you feel is to change what you are doing."
Rex Kocherhans

LightningMoments.com

learned that frequently after disappointment or a traumatic event, people withdraw from social life. This withdrawal leads to inactivity, inactivity leads to lower energy, and lower energy can eventually lead to depression. Our minds need stimulation to keep active. During the divorce, I had crawled back into bed to avoid dealing with the stress, and as a result, I simply didn't have the energy to get out; my comfort zone had become my bed. I discovered two simple tips to overcome depression and expand your comfort zone: First, change what you focus on. Second, action can elevate your mood naturally. With this direction, I developed the 10-Minute Challenge.

10-Minute Challenge

I decided to accept Dr. Kocherhans's challenge to expand my comfort zone. I would get out of bed and exercise for ten minutes every day, no matter how I felt, and I would do this for five consecutive days. The first day was incredibly difficult; I did not want to get out of bed. I took a moment to write down my feelings in a journal, and then I spent more than two hours praying for the strength to just get myself out of bed. I got myself onto the treadmill. I loathed every minute, and I kept looking at the timer. As soon as it ticked ten minutes, I was off the treadmill and back in bed, dead tired. My journaling that day expressed my exhaustion before and after exercise. I slept the rest of the day. The second day was a little easier—it took only one hour for me to pump myself up enough to get out of bed. Once the ten minutes were up, I was off to bed again. However, that day I lay in bed awake more than I slept. By the third day, I reached for my headphones and music. It took only half an hour to get out of bed and then out the door for a brisk walk around the neighborhood. I began reciting affirmations to the beat of the music while I walked, and the next thing I knew, it was fifteen minutes later! I had exceeded my goal. My journaling that day took a turn as well. I actually noticed an increase in energy twenty minutes after exercise, and I recorded this in my journal. Day after day, I accepted the challenge. More often than not, the ten minutes expanded, first to fifteen, then twenty, while the time I spent in bed began to decrease. Movement was magic; within a few short months, I had the energy to get out of bed.

What's keeping you from achieving your goals? It takes only ten minutes to find out. Discover the "10-Minute Challenge" activity in the "Knowledge in Action" section at the end of this chapter. Step out of your box, and expand your comfort zone.

Chapter 7
The Box, AKA ... Your Comfort Zone
Dare to step outside of your box

Knowledge in *Action*

LightningMoments.com

Expand Your Comfort Zone

Discover your obstacle, write it down and then identify actions you can take to expand your comfort zone. Record your feelings before your action, then perform the action for a minimum of ten minutes. Finally record your feelings after action. Watch yourself expand your comfort zone as you take courage and step outside of your box.

10-Minute Challenge	
Obstacle	
Feelings Before	
Action	
Feelings After	

CHAPTER 8

Seeking Peace

Peace Comes through Forgiveness

What is it that every human being earnestly seeks but rarely finds? During the years before my divorce was final, I learned to replace nonproductive thoughts with feelings of success and happiness, but still I felt that something was missing. Only one thing could help me feel whole again, and that would be peace.

Recently, I found myself going through our "important papers" file, and I discovered my old passport. The picture had been taken more than ten years earlier, and the passport had expired the previous year. I also found my recently updated passport in the file. Curious to see how much I had changed in ten years, I opened both to the photo page. My husband and I were surprised by the photo taken over a decade earlier. My eyes seemed lifeless and my skin dull, and although I was smiling in the photo, my face showed stress. We compared this photo to the one in my new passport. The difference was astonishing. I looked ten years younger in the new passport photo. It reflected a new light in my eyes, a more radiant, glowing smile.

I remember the day I had had the new passport photo taken. As the attendant snapped the photo, I could see my adoring husband out of the corner of my eye, smiling at me in the background. I blushed.

I also vividly remember the day the expired photo was taken—during one of the lowest points in my life. My former husband and I were separated but not yet divorced, and we were barely speaking to each other. When we did talk, the exchange usually ended in words of anger or disapproval. I felt unhappy and couldn't see a future for myself.

Over the years as I used the old passport, a number of individuals commented on the photo. They would examine the passport photo, look at me, and then look at the passport again, finally saying, "That does not even look like you!" At the time, I laughed it off. But now, looking at the photos side by side, I smiled at my husband and said, "That's what finding peace can do!"

My life, which had been such a wreck during the divorce, wore me out. Now, after years of controlling my thoughts, focusing on forgiveness, and letting go of past hurts, my face reflected the change: I had found peace.

If peace is what we seek, why is peace so hard to attain? Viktor Frankl was a Jewish psychiatrist held captive in a Nazi concentration camp for over three years. Starved, beaten, and persecuted, during his time as a prisoner, he used his skill as a psychiatrist to control his attitude. Because of his efforts with thought, he was able to maintain his strength and stamina. In his book *Man's Search for Meaning*, Frankl emphasizes this observation: even though his captors tried to break him by taking every freedom away from him, they could not take the most important thing—his freedom to manage his own attitude. In any circumstance, we have the right to choose how we react to any situation. Viktor Frankl did not allow the actions of others to affect his thoughts or influence his feelings. To me, he is a powerful example of someone who found peace in the midst of a terrible trial.

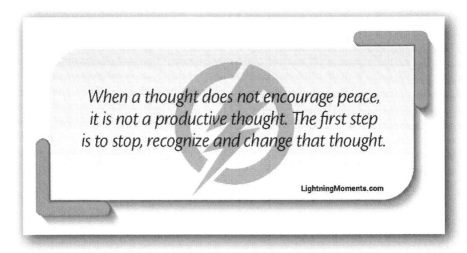

When a thought does not encourage peace, it is not a productive thought. The first step is to stop, recognize and change that thought.

LightningMoments.com

All productive thoughts will promote feelings of peace. So when a thought does not encourage feelings of peace, it is not a productive thought. The first step is to stop, recognize, and change that thought.

Seeking Peace

Each story within this book is a layer. As I record each story, I often wonder why it took many years and many experiences for me to learn each of these tools and put them into consistent action. I share with you a story about my personal motto, one that I developed to survive motherhood and used personally as I learned about forgiveness.

During the years of my previous marriage, I often felt unloved. Thoughts of loss tormented me each day. Torn by these thoughts and struggling with depression, I found it difficult to get out of bed for more than twenty minutes at a time. As a mom, I felt overwhelming responsibility for my family; they were young and needed my guidance. I honestly enjoyed being a mom, but the personal struggles of uselessness were real. Now, years later, I can look back on the experience of the divorce and see that when I focused my thoughts on my children and their needs, it became easier for me to get out of bed and perform the daily tasks. Service gave me something to live for.

However, at that time, I habitually focused on nonproductive thoughts of personal loss. Feeling sad and unimportant, I simply could not function. I had forgotten to live my own motto.

I created it when my family was very young to help the children focus on what they could do instead of what they didn't have. "Remember, it's all in the attitude... *Make* it a great day!" I affirmed this motto day in and day out—with my kids, with their friends, with anyone I ever met. Many times, friends and family have said to me, "I was in a difficult situation and your motto came to mind. 'It's all in the attitude...*Make* it a great day!' So I mustered the strength, and I just made myself do it."

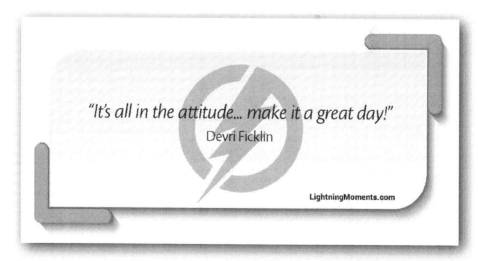

"It's all in the attitude... make it a great day!"
Devri Ficklin

LightningMoments.com

It was embarrassing to have others living my motto, yet I had given up when going through an emotionally demanding situation! I believed in the power of my motto, but daily I failed to follow it. I didn't know what the outcome of the divorce would be. I desperately searched for something but did not know what. It wasn't until years later that I discovered what I was seeking: peace.

Learning to Forgive

One of the most freeing experiences of my life came after my divorce, when I finally truly forgave my former husband and, more importantly, learned to forgive myself. Disappointed in my unsuccessful efforts to maintain the marriage, angry that he and I could not weather the storm and make our marriage work, I felt hurt and unforgiving. I never imagined that our children would experience a broken family or that there would be years of struggle that provoked such bitterness.

One day during the separation process, I ran into a friend at the grocery store. It had been over nine years since we had last seen each other. The first words out of her mouth were that she and her husband had recently divorced. I remained silent. This friend had no idea that my husband and I were separated at the time, but our divorce was not yet final. The conversation quickly centered on everything her former husband had done—the infractions, the injustices to both her and her children. Yes, I heard a sad tale, an entire dirty-laundry list of things he had done wrong. My heart ached for her. I understood her disappointment. Feeling abandoned and unloved, she exuded resentment and hostility. This proved to be another Lightning Moment, because as I walked away from her that day, I decided that I did not want to fall into the divorced-woman stereotype: bitter, angry, and alone.

Avoiding the "Bitterness Trap"

Actually *living* my motto—"It's all in the attitude…*Make* it a great day!"—I began to cultivate each thought, staying away from anything centered on loss or injustice. I would not allow myself to become bitter. Through much prayer, I focused on changing the destructive thoughts that often roamed through my mind. Each time a nonproductive thought about my former husband or the pending divorce entered my mind, I used the CC&3Rs—as many times as needed each day! I also began to study the effects of forgiveness and revenge. I was truly seeking peace.

Forgiveness or Revenge...You Choose

While sitting on the lawn at a chapel in Stratford-upon-Avon in England, I listened to the beautiful carol of the bells as they pealed for over thirty minutes. The sound was magnificent, and I felt their energy resonate through my entire being! My mother and I were in the United Kingdom, finishing up a trip of a lifetime: three weeks exploring the splendor of England, Wales, Ireland, and Scotland. On the lawn, I savored each event of the incredible experience. Down by the river, not far from where I sat, I observed a young family. As the father swung the children around one after another, I could hear their squeals of delight. Their mother was laughing and chasing them as they wobbled to and fro after each turn. I could hear their joy singing as they called, "Again, Daddy! Again, please!" Reality began to settle. I felt the dread of returning to the shackles of real life and the impending divorce.

I found myself standing at the crossroads of life. I had a choice: I could continue on my current road of stalling the divorce and prolonging the sadness that would lead to bitterness and revenge, or I could choose to take the road of peace. I had avoided the decision in hopes of dodging the consequences. The dark road ahead would be made of choices, and I would have to take a step into the unknown before my path would lighten. But I knew I couldn't survive much longer by remaining the same.

Which road would I choose? I began to pray mightily that I could feel peace as I embarked on a journey into the unknown. I had no idea where the road would take me, or what difficulties were waiting for me when I returned home. At that moment, the spirit of peace spoke to my soul, reminding me that for twenty-six days I had lived each day to the fullest, in complete happiness. Taking this trip to England had been like a step in the dark for me—completely out of my comfort zone. I left my daughter and son thousands of miles away with family members in America as I explored an unknown countryside, driving on the left side of the road for the first time, taking the underground tube, just me and my mom. Yes, this definitely was outside of my box. And during the entire visit, I had not crawled into my bed and cried, as I usually did when I felt the stress of life. For twenty-six days, I hadn't cried or crawled into bed, nor had I felt like doing it. Seriously, in twenty-six days, I hadn't cried even one tiny tear—a feat I had not accomplished in over five years of separation!

Peace Comes through Forgiveness; Let It Go!

It was another Lightning Moment. As reality set in, the direction of my life seemed to change for the better. I would be all right; focused on faith and service to others, I could live a fulfilling life as a single mom. I recognized the nonproductive effects that a long, drawn-out separation and divorce were having on my life and the lives of our children. Anger was hampering my growth. At that moment, I chose to *let go* of the anger. I would forgive my former spouse for not being the husband I wanted, and I hoped that in time he would forgive me too. I acknowledged that neither of us needed to "win" in order for both of us to succeed. We were both better off alone than trying to build a dysfunctional life together. I also learned the importance of forgiving myself; accepting myself for who I am; and most important, loving myself. A burden lifted that day. With clarity, I moved forward. No longer afraid of what lay ahead, I had survived driving on the left side of the road—a huge deal! Happy, successful, and full of confidence, I had accomplished hard things. I knew I could survive anything.

With the decision made, I moved forward with my life. I found ways to serve my former husband and to serve others by letting go of petty grievances. I discovered that no one needed to be wrong for us both to be right, and even if the other person was not forgiving, forgiveness on my part was emotionally freeing! Service to others brings peace. Although the marriage would take another two years to dissolve, I began to build a happy, more successful life focused on forgiveness and service.

Seeking Peace—Getting over the "Bitterness Trap"

When people go through trials or challenges—especially those they perceive to be caused by other people—they often ask, "Why me?" Fixating on nonproductive thoughts can cause feelings of anger or bitterness. These nonproductive feelings can promote actions of revenge that can affect the quality of their lives and the lives of their loved ones. Add a nonproductive emotional connection, and it can create a vendetta, which can inspire out-of-control actions—such as an out of character action of a man physically pushing or hurting a family member out of emotional anger or the desire for revenge—that prompt friends and family to say, "I would have never believed they could do such a thing."

It's important to let go of hurt and to refuse to carry a grudge. Forgiveness is the most vital action for peace. The benefit of forgiveness affects the giver much more than it affects the receiver.

Through understanding, acceptance, and forgiveness of yourself and others, peace will come. Try following these steps:

- **Be kind even when it's not deserved.** Being disrespectful often causes collateral damage to unintended targets—such as hurting those who witness the interaction. Besides, you never know what struggles others are privately facing, so be kind and understanding.
- **Help others feel important.** When people are negative, it's usually because they are insecure.
- **Think of others.** Avoid taking things personally; typically, people are not out to get you. But if they are, protect yourself, and forgive them anyway.
- **Serve others.** Through service, you learn to accept differences and love others.
- **Forgive others.** Stuffed pain only hurts you. Let it go, and forgive others for what they have done—and for not being what you want them to be.
- **Forgive yourself, and then accept and love yourself!** Loving oneself is the most important.

Take a moment to complete the "Bitterness Trap" activity located in the "Knowledge in Action" section at the end of this chapter. Explore your feelings, who do you need to forgive, and why and how will you let it go?

Your Potential Within

Think of a time when you were facing a challenge yet still felt that no matter how it turned out, you would be all right. This sense of *being all right* brings a feeling of peace in the midst of many trials. The key in determining if a thought is productive or non-productive is to ask yourself, "Does this thought promote feelings of peace?"

Success will not be handed to you; work for it!

LightningMoments.com

Once you learn to forgive others and to accept and love yourself, you can finally begin to discover the person you are meant to be—your potential within. It's not what you *can* do; you already have greatness within you. You are destined for success. What makes the difference between success and failure is what you *will* do: your actions. Success will not be handed to you; work for it! You alone determine your destiny. As you learn no one has to lose in order for you to win, you will discover who you are.

Chapter 8
Seeking Peace
Peace Comes Through Forgiveness

Knowledge in *Action*

LightningMoments.com

Peace Comes Through Forgiveness

Explore your feelings to identify who you need to forgive, why and how you will forgive. Remember to include yourself.

"Bitterness Trap" Activity		
Who	**Why**	**How**

CHAPTER 9

The Daily Routine

Daily Action Determines Success

J ust weeks before the crucial request from Lauri, when I began working at Paul Mitchell Schools, an experience set me on a path to daily success. It was nearly noon. I had wasted the last five hours trying to get out of bed. I threw off the covers and thought, *This time I am going to do it.* But a tension headache pounded, and I quickly pulled the sheets back around my neck. I chastised myself once again. *How did I let life get to this point?* With a marriage tumbling out of control, I was unhappy, alone, and exhausted. I drifted off to sleep once again.

I glanced at the clock. Now it was 12:10 p.m. *This is ridiculous! It's after noon, and I am still in bed wasting my life away.* In anguish, I reached for the clock radio and turned it on. The music began to play, and I recognized an old favorite tune. Memories of a happier time flooded my mind, and I began thinking about how life used to be. I could see a happier time, filled with aspirations and goals. As the music continued to play, I felt the rhythm. My head began to bob, and my body gently swayed to the beat.

Suddenly, the words shouted out from deep within as I burst into singing the chorus. I was happy singing the song…Then it dawned on me. *Aspirations…that's it! I have none!* The thought continued to grow. *I love goals. But when was the last time I achieved a goal or even set one?* Focused on simply surviving a divorce, I had let the challenges of life run my day-to-day activities without any direction. I knew what I was missing. In excited desperation, I grabbed for a pen and a piece of paper and began to write. That day long ago, I developed what I call the Daily Routine. When put into action, this system helped me get through the tough divorce; it helped me accomplish goals while at the same time taking control of my day-to-day performance.

Years later, as the lightning strike interrupted my life, Don patiently listened to my woes on "one of those days." Pain radiated up and down my legs. While rubbing the muscles, I tried to explain my physical struggle. For several months, I had focused intensely and painfully on healing my body and mind physically. I worked my muscles each day without seeing the desired results. I had little energy left to move. Thoughts of sadness and loss clouded my mind.

"Sweetheart, look at your progress," Don said. "You can walk our entire street; that's more than you could do a few weeks ago! You have overcome tough challenges before, and this probably won't be the last." He placed his hand on my cheek. "Where's that fighter I know?"

I began to search within my mind, and again, Don was right! With the stress of recovery, I had neglected the system that helped me through the heartbreaking challenges so many years before. A light flickered within my brain, and I turned to Don with a spark of enthusiasm and said, "I know what I need: my Daily Routine!"

Each of us will face challenges that can seem overwhelming. The question is, "How do you keep moving forward when life interferes?" The Daily Routine can help you control your environment and sustain inspiration and forward movement on a daily basis, even when life seems to get in the way. Let me tell you the parable of the thermometer versus the thermostat—and explain how you can influence your environment.

The Thermometer versus the Thermostat

Understanding the function of a thermometer is simple. You use it to check the temperature; its purpose is to reflect its environment. Before the digital age, the thermometer had mercury within its core. This mercury would expand or contract based on the surrounding environment. If you placed the thermometer in the sun or in a hot car, the mercury would expand to reflect a higher temperature. If you placed the thermometer in snow or in cold water, the mercury within the core would contract and display the lower temperature.

The thermostat, on the other hand, rather than acclimating to the surrounding environment, has the potential to alter its environment. When the thermostat's dial is set to a predetermined temperature, the thermostat kicks the unit on and either cools or heats the area, depending on the desired outcome. The thermostat has the power to improve its environment, while the thermometer simply shows the current temperature. You have the power to choose. You can turn into a thermometer and only reflect your surroundings, or you can become a thermostat and improve your environment by setting and achieving goals and cultivating your potential. You may not be able to control what life hands you, but you can determine the way you react to what life hands you. Your Daily Routine can assist you in achieving your goals.

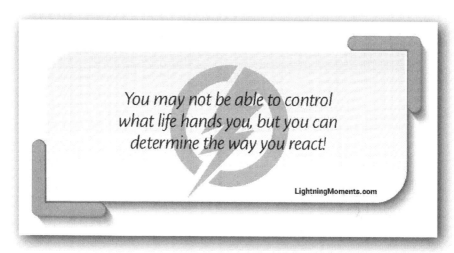

You may not be able to control what life hands you, but you can determine the way you react!

LightningMoments.com

Daily Routine

The Daily Routine is a ritual designed to assist in planning your day, focusing your energy, and increasing your productivity. It ensures that you stay on track and achieve great success. The Daily Routine can help you direct your attitude by focusing your thoughts, feelings, and actions.

The Daily Routine contains five main areas:

- Music
- Study
- Meditation
- Daily planning
- Exercise

Like a thermostat, the Daily Routine works best when you adapt the system to fit your individual needs. Let's discuss how to customize each area of the Daily Routine, beginning with music.

Music

Music is the art of sound. It expresses ideas and emotion through rhythm and beat. Most importantly, music can influence the natural energy within the body. I was traveling with a friend, and one morning she was having a very difficult time getting out of bed. I decided to conduct a music experiment. One of her favorite songs is "Don't Rain on My Parade" from the *Funny Girl* soundtrack. I put the music on and turned it up. Her first reaction was to pull her sheets over her head with an exasperated "Ugh." I wasn't deterred; I let the music continue to play. Before the second chorus, she was out of bed, singing and even dancing to the tune. That's the magic of music!

You have probably experienced this yourself: a tough day that is immediately turned around when your favorite song comes on the radio. One minute you were upset and frustrated, and the next thing you knew, you were swaying to the beat and had forgotten the stress of the day. Music can be used anytime to improve personal energy. This is why step one to the Daily Routine is music.

Music has the potential to influence emotion. Play music first thing upon awakening to influence your personal energy. Choose a theme song for your Daily Routine by identifying your music preference, the beat of a song, and a motivational message that best suits your needs.

Choosing Your Daily Routine Theme Song

First, create a playlist of songs that you love and to which you never tire listening. At this point, do not limit the list. Write down all of your favorite songs.

Now, choose a song with a beat that's based on your energy needs. To increase energy, choose a song with a beat that's faster than your natural heart rate. A resting heart rate is around sixty to eighty beats per minute. A song's beat can influence your heart rate and energy within your body. Your heartbeat can increase to match the tempo of a song. Choose the right beat, and within a few minutes, you will feel your energy increase.

Choose songs with motivational messages. The quickest way to achieve a goal is to surround yourself with productive thoughts about your goal and then connect these thoughts to music! You can choose the music you listen to. Rather than allowing a running stream of depressing lyrics, complaints, or criticism to occupy your mind, choose songs with inspirational messages.

The other day my husband groaned, "Ugh...I've got that song stuck in my head." And he began singing the irritating lyrics. I smiled and shook my head; I thought that was the end of that. A few minutes later, though, I noticed myself humming the same tune as the lyrics played over and over in my mind. I turned to him, exasperated. "Now that song is stuck in my head!" We both laughed.

If you are going to have a song stuck in your head, make it an inspirational one. Avoid any song with foul or degrading lyrics, because the negativity could influence your mind's or body's energy. Negative or crude music could have the potential to depress. For years, science has used music as therapy because of its ability to improve the body's natural energy. My personal experience with uplifting music or lyrics has shown me their ability to lift the mood. At times, I use an instrumental-only version of a song, which lets me repeat personalized affirmations to the music without the interruption of lyrics.

Look at your list of favorite songs. Repeat the words to the songs, and mark the ones with a *great* motivational message. Then, ask yourself, "Are there any songs on this list that need to be crossed off because of their message?" Stick with songs that possess a productive message.

Tips for Using Your Daily Routine Theme Songs
Now that you have your list of songs you can use the following success tips to inspire and motivate you:

- Download your chosen music, and then organize in playlists with your favorite songs in the following categories: morning wakeup, exercise, energy boost.
- Always keep the music close by for a quick pick-me-up.
- Listen to the music first thing upon awakening to increase your energy (even before you get out of bed, if necessary).
- Focus your thoughts, and repeat personal affirmations about your goals.
- Listen to the music anytime you need extra motivation.

Music can influence your natural energy and lift your mood. So turn on your chosen theme song, and within a few minutes, you too will begin swaying to the beat and singing to the music!

Study
Personal study can empower you to live what you believe by developing characteristics that emanate from within. But first, you need to uncover areas for your personal study. Do you know yourself? What do you believe or value?

A *value* is a set of beliefs or principles that influences behavior and can be described as a foundation that drives action. What values do you possess that influence your behavior? For example, you may value health and strength and therefore choose not to smoke because years of scientific testing show that smoking may be harmful for the lungs or heart.

Take a few minutes to identify characteristics you admire in a hero or a leader, either living or dead and then explore your own personal characteristics. Record the characteristics you would like to acquire or continue to develop on the "Desired Characteristics" activity that can be found in the "Knowledge in Action" section at the end of this chapter. In the second column of the activity sheet, identify the value or belief that drives or supports the behavior. In the third column, write the word *possess* if you already possess the characteristic, and write the word *acquire* if you would like to acquire the characteristic. In the far right column, write an action you can take to develop or improve the characteristic.

Identify Core Values

Take the time to assess and define each value or belief on your list. Group them into appropriate topics—for example, family, relationships, work, spiritual, health. Identify supporting actions, and finally identify your top three by asking yourself, "Which three values or beliefs are the most important to me?" These top three represent your core values. Record these top three on the activity sheet in the "Knowledge in Action" section at the end of this chapter. Although there may be many values on your list, building your goals around your top three can help you choose actions that support your values or help you prioritize decisions based on your values.

For example, if you chose "Spending time with family" or "Eating breakfast as a family each morning" as a characteristic, then family is an important value to you. However, if you stay up late after the kids go to bed and then you have a hard time getting up in the morning, you can include the action "Go to bed by 10:00 p.m."

Schedule Personal Study

Once you have identified desired characteristics, your top three core values, and the actions you can take to improve, you can use personal study time daily to improve yourself both spiritually and personally. Read articles and books or listen to motivational programs that develop those desired characteristics including leadership, integrity, and faith. Record what you have learned, including thoughts and feelings in either written or digital form. Whatever your beliefs may be, the stronger you are spiritually and personally, the stronger you will be in all areas of life. By taking care of yourself first, you have the energy to take care of others.

Meditation

Many people truly believe there's no way to control what happens to them. They resign themselves to just having rotten luck or to being victims of circumstance. A majority of people dwell on their nonproductive experiences. In a sense, dwelling on nonproductive experiences *is* a form of meditation. We have all heard the big question "Why me?" and its variations, "Why doesn't anything good ever happen to me?" and "Why does life have to be so difficult?" Individuals who fixate on negativity usually do seem to have more than their share of problems. It's true that some people are dealt more challenges than others. I'm not sure why, but it happens. I also believe the old adage "What you think about, you bring about." By dwelling on challenges, we often seem to get more than our share.

As I said before, you may not be able to control what life hands you, but you can determine the way you react to what life hands you. So if you think that something good (or, for that matter, something bad) is going to happen to you, you are probably right! Thoughts—both conscious and subconscious—can affect your surroundings. Your thoughts draw toward you the things you focus on. Choose to be the thermostat: take control of your environment by focusing your thoughts. As a nonproductive thought comes in your mind, choose to replace it with a productive thought. Personal strength comes as you focus your thoughts on gratitude. Prayer, meditation, and journaling are excellent ways to focus your thoughts.

The Higher Power of Meditation

There is a "higher power" in the universe. Whatever your spiritual belief, whether it be in God or another form, this higher power is ready and willing to serve you. Ask in faith and sincerity, and the universe will manifest into your life that which you ask. Take the time each day to meditate or pray. During meditation, find a quiet place and settle your mind. If you feel you will zone out for too long, set an alarm on your cell phone, and then relax. Share feelings of gratitude for all you have received, ask for the things you need, take a moment to listen, and look for ways you can serve or help others. Just a few minutes of meditation each day can promote peace, strength, and understanding.

One last tip on meditation. During the rare times when it is not practical to perform meditation or when you are not able to find a quiet place but you need the peace that can come from meditating, quieten your mind by focusing on productive thoughts and showing gratitude. This can help to improve your mind-set.

Keep a Gratitude Journal

After meditation, take a moment to record your feelings in a gratitude journal. Focus on the things you have to be grateful for, and look at the things you are blessed with in your life. Express gratitude for the kindness of others, and pay special attention to the tender mercies—little events that bring you peace or happiness throughout the day. Document your feelings as you focus your writing on productive thoughts. Anytime you feel discouraged or need a boost, review the many wonderful experiences recorded in your journal.

Express gratitude for the kindness of others.

LightningMoments.com

Recently, I experienced a particularly stressful day. I needed to make a phone call to someone I really like, but who is sometimes difficult to work with. Her actions were affecting my business, and they could not be ignored. Anyone who knows me understands I do not like confrontation. I wanted to avoid the difficult situation but knew that was impossible. Instead, I sat in my bedroom in what I call the "prayer chair" and took a moment to contemplate the imminent conversation before making the crucial call. On the ottoman next to the chair was an old journal. I picked it up and began to thumb through the pages. My eyes landed on an entry I had made many years before, recording my memories of another very stressful day and the strength I felt as I learned to focus on productive thinking—more specifically, how my thoughts in a given situation could influence the outcome. I recognized through reading this entry that my present thoughts were nonproductive and were negatively influencing the outcome. They were based on the fear of change. Using CC&3Rs, I was able to release the nonproductive thoughts, and I found inspiration as I focused on the "doors of opportunity" that were opening for both my husband and me. Yes, changes would be needed. However, by changing my thoughts from ones of fear to ones of opportunity, I found the courage, picked up the phone, and made the difficult call. Ten minutes later, I recorded thoughts of gratitude for facing my fear and making the call. That experience began a relationship built on trust.

Take the time to write and then reread the messages of determination and inspiration documented in your gratitude journal.

Daily Planning

The simple act of daily planning can help you focus on your goals, manage your day, and stay on task. Daily planning is an energizing combination of task management and time management that includes a daily schedule, a list of the goals you would like to accomplish, and a focus for the day that supports your goals. A daily schedule that includes a goal review can help you keep your eye on the target. The steps required to achieve your goal may change along the way, but eventually, with a little stretching and with one completed task at a time, victory is yours.

Keep your eye on the target!

LightningMoments.com

Create a Daily-Tasks List

Review your daily To-Do list and divide it into Have to Dos, Important to Dos, and Goals:

- **Have to Dos:** These are items that demand accomplishment today. Schedule these Have to Dos directly into your day. Where possible, include a time frame for the activity. Complete your top three Have-to-Do tasks first. Have to Dos include tasks that you *will do* today—and that you will not go to bed tonight until you've completed. I focus on completing these early in the day, so that I am not pulling late nights to finish them.
- **Important to Dos:** These are things that you can do today, if you have time. Use these items to fill in empty spaces of time throughout the day. As you schedule these items into your day, plan a time frame to keep you on track and focused.
- **Goals:** Schedule a minimum of one item into the Have to Dos that will move you toward achieving your goals. Adding two or three will get you to the achievement of your goals quicker. I often include personal goals in my top three Have to Dos.

As the day progresses, complete the tasks and mark them off the list. The goal is to complete all of the day's Have-to-Do tasks and, if possible, a few of the Important-to-Do tasks.

Daily Focus

Once you have planned your daily schedule, choose a daily focus that supports your goals. Then write this focus into an affirmation that is personal. Write it in the present

Complete one task at a time; victory is yours!

LightningMoments.com

tense, and make sure it contains productive linking words. Here is an example of one of my focus affirmations: "I am a woman of strength and character. I successfully accomplish all planned tasks."

Exercise

You must expend energy in order to increase energy. Are you feeling tired or sluggish? Exercise is one of the quickest ways to increase your energy. Even though I understand the benefits of exercise, it's still a daily struggle for me to get my body moving. I've found that journaling my feelings before and after exercising helps me recognize the personal benefits of regular exercise. I absolutely feel a difference on the days I choose not to exercise; my body and mind function more slowly. Luckily for me, more often than not, I choose exercise, and it often expands into fifteen to thirty minutes. Exercising honestly feels amazing!

Track your exercise using an exercise log. Review it weekly to inspire and motivate continued action. You will find a sample "Energy and Exercise Log" in the "Knowledge in Action" section at the end of this chapter.

Music and Exercise

Annie, a Cross Kick instructor, shared with me that the types of music she plays during a workout session have a definite influence on how the individuals she's training work out. When she plays fast-paced music with a strong beat, they tend to work longer and with more intensity. She said that during exercise, class members often match their movement with the beat of the song without realizing it.

In this chapter, you created a playlist of your favorite songs. Now choose a mixture of upbeat songs you love to listen to, and create an exercise list. After I created my favorite exercise-music playlist, I recorded myself reciting personal affirmations throughout the songs. I use this affirmation playlist to motivate myself during exercise.

Managing Your Daily Routine

I am not typically a morning person, but somehow after years of performing the Daily Routine, I have become a morning person. Performing the Daily Routine helps me to manage mornings by creating a path for daily success. On days when time is short, your Daily Routine can take as little as fifteen minutes; when time permits, it can be a full hour. Let's discuss how this is accomplished.

Minutes to Win It!—Short Version (Fifteen Minutes)

Short on time? Listen to your theme song as you get dressed to exercise. Next, review your daily schedule; then, choose a focus while you exercise for ten minutes. End the Daily Routine with a few minutes of meditation and gratitude. Save time by performing the study segment via a podcast or motivational CD or video while you shower and get dressed for the day.

Power Hour—Long Version (Sixty Minutes)

For longer segments, follow the Daily Routine in the order shown below, giving each segment the time needed to complete the tasks. Here is a suggested breakdown:

- Music—five minutes
- Study—ten minutes
- Meditation—five minutes
- Daily planning—ten minutes
- Exercise—thirty minutes

Creating Your Daily Routine

Throughout this book, you have discovered tools and techniques to assist you in creating an action plan. The final step is to put it all together by formulating your Daily Routine. Use the "Daily Routine, Gratitude Journal, Energy and Exercise Log" activity sheets in the "Knowledge in Action" section at the end of this chapter to help you customize a Daily Routine.

Like the thermostat, you have now learned important systems to take control of your environment. Keep moving forward, and achieve your goals by performing the Daily Routine.

Chapter 9
The Daily Routine
Daily Action Determines Success

Knowledge in *Action*

LightningMoments.com

Daily Action Determines Success

In the far left column identify personal characteristics or characteristics you admire in a hero or a leader, either living or dead. Next, identify the value or belief that drives or supports the behavior. In the third column record the word "Possess" if you already possess the characteristic, and "Acquire" if you would like to acquire the characteristic. In the far right column write an action you can take to develop or improve the characteristic. Then group the characteristics into topics and identify your top three values. Finally, record the items you would like to learn, develop or improve in the space provided.

Desirable Characteristics			
Characteristic	Value	Possess or Acquire	Actions to Develop or Improve

My Top 3 Values (Core Values)
1
2
3

Things I will learn, develop or improve:

Chapter 9
The Daily Routine
Daily Action Determines Success

Knowledge in *Action*

LightningMoments.com

Daily Action Determines Success

Customize a Daily Routine to fit your needs, and then perform the routine daily to keep you on track and moving toward goal achievement.

Daily Routine	
Daily Focus:	**Date:**
Have to Dos:	Appointments
1	
2	
3	
Important To Do's:	
Additional Items:	

For personal/study time today I will:

Chapter 9
The Daily Routine
Daily Action Determines Success

Knowledge in *Action*

LightningMoments.com

Daily Action Determines Success

Track your exercise using an exercise log. Record how you feel before and after exercise and then measure the increased energy you receive as you move your body — this will inspire continued dedication. Review your successes weekly and set intentional goals to motivate your continued action. Celebrate each and every achievement!

Gratitude Journal
Date:

Energy and Exercise Log
The two most powerful words "I am..." — write a simple affirmation.
Personal Goals Today: ☐ ☐ ☐

Fitness Activity	Minutes	Intensity

Before exercising I felt:
20 minutes after exercising I feel:
For personal/study time today I will:

CHAPTER 10

Imperfection or a Work of Art

Get "Back on Track" when Life Gets in the Way

For over a year, I struggled with how to write the final chapter of this book—with how to tie the information together in a way that would inspire you to put it into action. With the key points organized for the final chapter, I experienced for the first time what could be described as writer's block: the words just were not coming. Day after day, I reordered a few of the sentences but did not love the outcome. Days turned into weeks. Then one day the words came in another Lightning Moment.

On a very typical morning at five o'clock, I rolled over to my husband's side of the bed as he rose for the day. I snuggled in and easily fell back to sleep. Suddenly confused, I found myself standing by the side of the bed. Half asleep, I couldn't figure out why I had jumped from the bed so quickly. A bombardment of loud thuds and thumps followed. I heard my husband yell from the other room as he came running down the hall. "Devri, are you all right?"

At that moment, something I recognized as a cinder block came crashing through the outside wall of the house, landing on the carpet two feet from where I stood. A spray of concrete and wallboard filled the room and spilled into the hall as I choked on the smoke and dust. *It's a tornado!* I thought, just as Don came running in the room. Dazed, I reassured him, "I am fine!"

He turned and hurried down the hall toward the backyard, yelling, "Call nine one one!" I lunged for the phone and began to dial but then realized there was no dial tone. I headed for the door to use the phone in another room but quickly saw that I wasn't properly dressed. Stopping abruptly, I turned and reached for the clothes I had laid on the chair the previous night; they were now covered with the debris from the destruction.

My eyes went to the cement-filled cinder block that lay on the floor fifteen inches inside the room and to a two-foot-by-two-foot hole that had been ripped through the bedroom wall, just below the window. I stared at torn pieces of insulation, exposed wiring, and the framing lumber hanging in the gaping hole that now led directly to our backyard. The bloody, scratched legs of a man I did not recognize suddenly walked past the hole in the wall. Outside, I heard shouting.

What are strange people doing in my backyard yelling? I thought, as I quickly threw on my clothes and ran toward the backyard.

"You guys all right?" Don called out. "Is there anyone else in the car?" He'd arrived in the backyard just in time to see two teenagers drop out of the shattered back window of a blue sports car. It was lying on its passenger side, half its original size, wedged into the ten-foot hole it had created in our south block wall. The car's engine was still smoking, and dust was filling the air. Don quickly grabbed the kitchen phone. Luckily, it worked, and he called 911 for help.

An emotional whirlwind followed. Over the next six hours, police pieced together the events of the accident. Speed played a major role in the accident, as the blue sports car traveling southbound on the road behind our house bottomed out and the driver lost control. The driver overcorrected and threw the car into a roll, directly into our yard. The car smashed through the back wall, changed directions during the roll, and landed facing southbound on the opposite wall, embedded in the block-wall fence. The accident catapulted a cement-filled cinder block through the walls of our home—into the room where I peacefully slept and the adjoining bathroom.

Fortunately, two teenage passengers walked away from the accident with only minor cuts and bruises. The driver was taken by ambulance to the trauma center in critical condition. He suffered serious damage to every area of his body except his head. He suffered a ripped aortic valve, shattered hip and shoulder, broken leg, torn liver, and ruptured spleen. Weeks later, we learned from his family that although he survived the crash, he would need constant medical care for the rest of his life.

There is simply no way to explain the emotions you experience during and after an event like this. Our initial concern was for the well-being of the individuals in the car. Once their needs were taken care of, our focus turned to the physical devastation of our property. The damage resembled something you'd see in a photo of a war-torn country. It looked as if a bomb had detonated in our backyard, ripping massive holes in the side of our house. Our beautiful home had experienced extensive damage. The concrete-reinforced cinder block from the fence had flown more than fifty feet, penetrating the exterior walls of our home in several locations and actually ripping cavernous holes through the exterior wall and into the master bedroom and bath. In other areas, the cinder block was embedded in the walls like stone claws, actually bowing walls inside the home as it pushed the framework out of place. The yard was littered with nearly unrecognizable pieces from the car: fenders, lights, and wheels that had been smashed during the collision. Concrete, rocks, cinder block, and glass from the car covered the patio, where the car had come to rest after hitting the back of our home; some large blocks had even made their way into the front yard.

The widespread damage included the roof, sixty feet of the back wall, exposed electrical lines, and insulation. Even the phone line in the bedroom was snapped in half. Along the south side of the home, we discovered the bent and twisted ten-foot-by-two-foot metal railing that had been violently ripped from the east block-wall fence as the car broke through the rebar- and cement- reinforced cinder-block wall. The sheer force of the crash ripped the metal railing and catapulted it up and over the house; it landed ninety feet from its original starting place against the south wall. Small pieces of the railing were flung everywhere. As the large railing landed on the side of the home, the metal gouged a deep crevice into the south block wall.

We recognized a tender mercy from heaven that day, as both Don and I were in vulnerable positions when the car hit the wall. The back of our home received massive damage from chunks of cement, cinder block, and metal that peppered the stucco surrounding the wall and windows. I had jumped to a standing position just a few feet away from the large bedroom window as the car crashed through the block-wall fence. Accident debris also embedded itself within the stucco wall surrounding the much larger windows, just inches from where Don sat in the family room, down the hall. Miraculously, absolutely nothing—metal, cinder block, or cement—had shattered or even cracked the long wall of windows that spanned the back wall of our home, so close to where both Don and I had been positioned.

Reliving the Ordeal

Five days later, I was healthy and alive, having cheated death once again. Yet despite my good fortune, I was struggling. It started as a difficult morning. I had a hard time waking up, which was unusual for me; since marrying Don ten years earlier, I had incorporated his early-morning habits. I pushed myself, threw back the covers, and climbed out of bed. I moved slowly around the bed and pulled up the shade to let in the morning sun. I gazed up the hill to the back wall—a cinder-block fence, now patched with plywood. I saw the pitted surface from embedded accident debris.

My thoughts wandered. *How will we ever get the house back to normal?* Anger flared at the thoughtless kid showing off in his new sports car. Tension began to build in my neck. I rolled my shoulders, stretched my neck from side to side, and then took a deep breath. I tried not to concentrate on the challenges of fixing the broken fence and our damaged home. I tried not to think of what could have been.

But any noise, large or small, sent my heart racing with a rush of adrenaline. I heard a motorcycle coming up the back road, and I thought *He's going too fast. He's so stupid! Doesn't he know how dangerous that is?* Anxiety enveloped my chest, and I dropped to my knees, wrapping my arms around my shoulders. Crying soon gave way to sobs, as I remembered the frightening experience. The tears continued, uncontrollable. I crawled back into bed and pulled the covers over my head.

Nearly an hour later, I pushed myself to get out of bed again and walked into my office. Surely, work would help. First, it was simply opening and reading e-mails and sending a few replies. Next, I reached for a manual I was supposed to review. After reading a page or two, I realized that my thoughts were scattered, and I was having trouble focusing. Suddenly, I heard another noise, and immediately the adrenaline pumped into my system. My heart began to beat rapidly as visions filled my mind of a car barreling down the hill toward our home. *What is that?* I panicked, and then I recognized the noise. The air conditioner had just kicked on, and the pressure of the air forced the bedroom door closed, a familiar sound that often rippled through the house.

Looking to find a way out of the emotional doom, I called Don. He has a way of getting me off the ledge. We talked a few minutes, and then he said, "Sweetheart, I'm sorry, but I need to get back to work. As soon as I get a chance, I will stop by."

"I am doing much better," I assured him, not wanting to worry him. We hung up the phone, but my tears slowly began again. Another hour passed. Next, I sent a text to my son, hoping he could stop by for a few minutes with the grandkids. After twenty minutes with no response, as a last resort I reached out to my daughter, Tajia, who lived in another state. I began to explain to her the emotional turmoil, and the tears began to flow once again. "Oh...the house...my work...stupid drivers. There is so much to do. Deadlines...revision...demolition. I have no energy to do it."

She patiently listened and then said, "So what's your plan today?"

"That's the problem," I cried. "There's *so* much to do; I can't figure it out!"

"OK...Let's talk about it. Mom, what *can* you do? Have you listened to your music today? What are your top-three goals to accomplish today? Have you studied or read anything today?" She quickly reviewed the steps to the Daily Routine, the system I had created more than fifteen years earlier.

"Tajia, you are correct!" Realization set in. I had risen from bed that morning and missed completing my Daily Routine. In fact, for more than five days, I had ignored putting the Daily Routine into practice. Within minutes, Tajia helped me focus productive thoughts on what I could accomplish and reminded me of the importance of "letting it go" as we formulated a plan to accomplish the tasks needed for the day. Immediately, the cloud began to lift. Having created the Daily Routine years before to get through the divorce, you'd think I would remember its importance! But when "lightning" struck once again, I lost focus and allowed the old habits to return. Finally, realizing my thoughts had gotten out of control and the anxiety was stress induced, I quickly put the routine into action. By focusing my thoughts, seeking peace through forgiveness, and putting the Daily Routine into action, I got my life back on track. My energy returned, and I rapidly moved toward goal achievement.

Direct Where "Your Lightning" Will Strike

During a second call later that day, my daughter and I discussed how ironic it was that something so emotionally frightening as a car crashing through your yard and catapulting cinder block into the walls of your home where you lay sleeping could actually be a blessing in disguise.

How could that be possible? Yet, this experience became the final inspiration that would tie together each tool within this book, a final message that struck quickly, like a bolt out of the blue. Unharnessed, lightning can destroy its environment; however, it also has the power for renewal. The earth begins to rebuild immediately after the strike, and often it comes back stronger and more beautiful than before. By following the systems in this book, in a sense I became the lightning. Within minutes of harnessing personal energy with a plan in hand, I directed where the power of the lightning would go, and I overcame a flood of devastating emotions. It felt good to be "back on track"!

The Greatest Tragedy

Have you ever experienced a moment when the voice inside your head whispers, *You can't do that...You're not good enough*? If so, you are not alone. Dr. Kocherhans shared with me that feeling "not good enough" ranked among the top of his patients' list of complaints.

Often we hit the snooze button to silence the voice deep within, hoping it will go away. However, thoughts or feelings stuffed deep within never go away. It takes focused energy to overcome these thoughts and realize the importance of the power you possess. Belief in self comes through doing; learn to harness personal power. Step outside of your comfort zone; then, with consistent effort, focus your thoughts, seek peace through forgiveness, create a daily routine, and put your plan into action. You can direct where your lightning will strike.

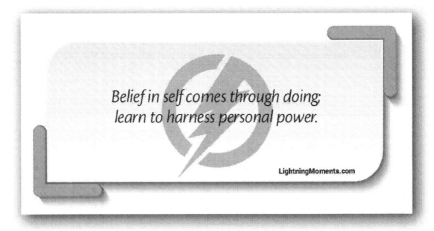

Belief in self comes through doing; learn to harness personal power.

LightningMoments.com

The greatest tragedy in life would be to discover at its end that you had "stuffed" your own personal power and never really lived. This book has come full circle, and I ask you again, "If today were your last, how would you spend your time?"

As I healed after the lightning strike, I took time to reflect on life. My thoughts were not about projects at work or deadlines or personal possessions. I filled my mind with happy memories of family and friends, with goals, and with dreams I had put off until "someday." Imagine that these were your last days. Would you be satisfied with your accomplishments? Are you honestly living the life you want remembered? I took a hard look at myself and discovered that I wasn't, and I made the decision to live "a life of no regrets"!

Every morning I thank the Lord for the blessing of another day on this incredible earth. I live each day with faith, courage, and determination. I never allow the shallowness of others to inhibit my happiness. I celebrate each small victory as I check the items off my list. I am creating the life I want remembered!

Through my literal Lightning Moment, I learned to change "Someday, I will…" to "Today, I am…" You alone control who you are and what you will become, and you have the power to create your own Lightning Moments.

Create "Lightning Moments" Every Day

I never dreamed I would be grateful for the experience of being struck by lightning, but I am. I will never be 100 percent healed from the strike, but this event was a pivotal moment in my life because it propelled me into action. I looked inward and faced my own mortality. At times, when life has not gone in the direction I desired, giving up would have been easy—and no one would blame me. But instead of giving in, I chose to focus my thoughts, feelings, and action on living the highest quality of life I can construct. It's definitely not perfect, but it's my life, and I love it! Through daily action, I now live the life of my dreams. I create Lightning Moments every day!

So, what is your Lightning Moment? Ask yourself, *Have I ever put off working toward a dream? Am I waiting for the right time, or until I perfect a specific trait or talent?* If the answer is yes, this may be your stumbling block. Turn your challenges into stepping stones on your road to greatness. The fact is, you will never be perfect, and you can always improve. Identify where you are now, determine what you need to do or learn in order to become what you desire, and then create a step-by-step plan that will help you achieve your goal.

My objective for this book is not for you to finish reading, think, "Wow, this is a really good story," and then place the book back on the shelf with the other books you've read. If you do nothing with this information, the message is lost. The purpose of sharing this story is to inspire you to *become the lightning*. Plan time to review your notes, complete the activities, and identify areas for growth. Reread the chapters as needed, and customize the information to fit your needs as you create a personal

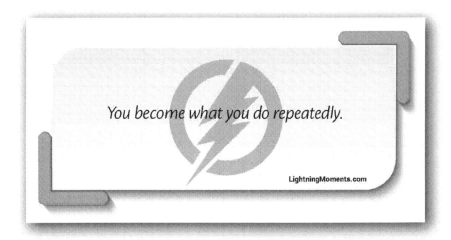

You become what you do repeatedly.

LightningMoments.com

strategy to improve your life. Avoid *waiting for lightning to strike* before you make important changes in your life; begin your personal quest for success.

Achieve your goals through these three simple steps:

- You are the master of your thoughts; focus them!
- Peace comes through forgiveness; let it go!
- Daily action determines success; plan, then do!

You become what you do repeatedly.

Create your own Lightning Moment. Focus your thought; create your reality. Then let it go: embark on the journey of peace through forgiveness, and make each day count. Life is waiting; it's your time to shine. The next step is yours; take it *now!*

Stay in the know, connect with us:

Are you interested in additional tools and tips to help you achieve success? Do you want to be notified as soon as the next book is released? Stay connected with us by visiting the www.LightningMoments.com website and signing up for our newsletter.

Book Devri for Your Next Event

Contact us today with your specific need, and have a customized training or workshop created that will inspire and motivate your large or small group. Request more information at www.LightningMoments.com.

Free 10-Minute Challenge ePacket

Are you ready to take control of your life? Your dreams are just a *click* away...

Check out our blog, and sign up for the *free* 10-Minute Challenge ePacket at www.LightningMoments.com.

Free *Lightning Moments* Membership

When you become an exclusive *Lightning Moments* member, you can download additional copies of your favorite *Lightning Moments* self-improvement tools at www.LightningMoments.com.

 Lightning Moments,   Lightning Moments

Made in the USA
San Bernardino, CA
13 September 2017